GOYA

JOSÉ GUDIOL

GOYA

EDICIONES POLÍGRAFA, S. A.

© *1986 Ediciones Polígrafa, S. A.*
Balmes, 54 - 08007 BARCELONA (Spain)

Translation by Kenneth Lyons

I.S.B.N.: 84-343-0464-3
Dep. Legal: B. 19.261 - 1986 (Printed in Spain)

Printed in Spain by La Polígrafa, S. A. - Parets del Vallès - Barcelona

CONTENTS

Foreword

Francisco Goya is a universal figure of Spanish art, one of its greatest figures, at least in the immense breadth of his range, whether in iconography or in technique, in expression or in image. Goya was endowed with a very rare gift for the interpretation and communication of plastic values, but also for the discovery and re-creation of beauty and human meaning in the most arid elements of nature. His inexhaustible vitality enabled him to make interesting any type of pictorial or graphic representation, presenting with equal intensity the terrible and the dramatic, or infusing depth into the banal and superficial themes which at times — above all at the beginning of his career as a Court painter — were demanded of him. Goya, moreover, since he lived between two periods and two worlds, the affected charms of Rococo and the early days of Romanticism, with the first stirrings of Expressionism, is a key figure in the genesis of contemporary European art.

He is important not only as an artist, but also as a man. Moved by a superhuman energy, he succeeded in more than making up for any defect in his physical nature. He was born and developed in a poor, backward world, surrounded by an exhausted, decadent society, in which very few individuals — throughout his existence — could provide him with relative friendship and comprehension. He only survived thanks to his tremendous vitality, which never left him, in sickness, old age or exile. He weathered the perils of a poor and stormy youth and his violent and passionate temperament evaded the temptations of the easy life he could have led by exploiting his success at a Court where he was only asked to provide a showy, superficial art, which his natural gifts as a colourist enabled him to produce without effort. He overcame his congenital fear of poverty, but he did not succumb to the temptations of material ambition or avarice, for his fidelity to the interior drive that gave rise to each of the varied facets of his work was always the main force in his life, if not the only one.

His instinctive capacity for discovering new techniques and expressive devices — Goya was never either an intellectual or an experimenter in the sense in which those terms are understood today — must astonish us more, if possible, than the flexibility of his spirit in covering the widest spheres of existence and fantasy, the latter being looked on as an interpretation of the former rather than a flight from it. Goya the painter of formless clots at the beginning of the 19th century, Goya the insuperable Expressionist of the "black paintings", or even as early as the tremendous details of the fresco of San Antonio de la Florida, reserves the greatest surprises in these domains, in which he holds sway with the same incomparable mastery as in his apparently most academic portraits or in his charming tapestry cartoons. For he always preserves the unity emanating from his powerful personality, which emerges through the centuries, formed in happy, decadent periods or in others as tragic as the days of the Napoleonic invasion, with its aftermath of crimes and violence of every kind.

The unity and the double breadth of Goya — in theme and procedure, in formula and spirit — leap to the eye in the pages of this book, animated by his hard — yet at the same time gay and caustic — temperament, as reflected in his letters, and also animated by the habit of genius, of which he was fully conscious in his youth, as we can see in the episode of his rebellion against Bayeu's judgment in the matter of the paintings for El Pilar.

The better to reveal and explain his personality, we have included phrases and paragraphs taken from Goya's letters and other writings, which have hitherto been only partially and fragmentarily published; the total publication of these important texts is indispensable and urgent.

Childhood, education and first commissions (1746-1774)

Goya's parents, José Goya and Engracia Lucientes, were citizens of Zaragoza. His paternal grandfather, Pedro, a scribe by profession, was of Basque origin. Goya's father was a gilder with his own workshop, a modest craftsman of limited income of whom nothing further is known. His obituary notice in the parish records for 1781 tells us no more than that "he made no will since he had nothing". The artist's mother was descended from some poor country gentry with a house and land in Fuendetodos, a village in one of the most desolate regions of Aragon. It was here that Francisco Goya was born on the 30th March 1746, in a small two-storeyed house with one passage, still miraculously standing, on a mean, winding street which is a quagmire in winter and a dust-track in summer. It is not known why Goya's mother was in Fuendetodos at the time. Very soon she returned to Zaragoza, the town in which the future painter was to spend his childhood and the early years of his youth.

Of Goya's childhood we have only the evidence of oral tradition. His earliest education was at the school of Father Joaquín, where he established a lasting friendship with a fellow-pupil, Martín Zapater, giving rise over the years to a copious correspondence, from which one hundred and thirty-two letters survive; these not only provide us with biographical data of considerable interest, but also reveal to us something of Goya's spontaneous character and personality. Goya also attended the school of drawing founded in 1714 by the sculptor Juan Ramírez. At the age of twelve or thirteen, he was apprenticed in the workshop of José Luzán, a painter who devoted himself to the production of the conventional religious works in demand at the time. The work of a painter-apprentice included the preparation of the colours and canvases, exercises in drawing from life and copying engravings. A workshop such as José Luzán's would have offered a satisfactory training in the technique of the painter's craft. The duration of a painter's apprenticeship was ordinarily four years.

Fig. 1   Goya's earliest known works, some paintings of a reliquary for the parish church of Fuendetodos, destroyed in 1936, show the influence of Luzán, and also of Antonio González Velázquez. The most probable supposition is that they were done some time towards the end of his apprenticeship, around 1762. The extraordinary power of these images indicates a lively and vigorous temperament, and they introduce certain characteristic types that were to recur in subsequent works.

The first positively datable reference to Goya establishes his presence in Madrid in 1763, at the age of seventeen. Charles Yriarte, one of Goya's first biographers, records the picturesque story of the painter's journey: "Goya's youth was wild and stormy;... ...he had to leave his native town, after a bloody encounter in which three men were left lying on the scene of the fight. His family hid him for some time and afterwards furnished him with the means to go to Madrid...".

In these years the Spanish capital was enjoying a period of increasing economic prosperity under the absolute but enlightened rule of Carlos III, a good king and a cultivated man. After the completion of the new Royal Palace and numerous churches and mansions, Madrid was experiencing for the moment an artistic boom, in which the painters were playing a leading role. To decorate the ceiling of the new royal residence, Corrado Giaquinto (1703-1765) was brought from Italy to Spain, and the works he executed there between 1753 and 1762 were to exercise a decisive influence on the Madrid school. Anton Raphael Mengs, born in Aussig (Bohemia) in 1728, arrived in Madrid in 1761, bringing to Spain the new ideas of Academicism and Neo-Classicism. In 1766 he was appointed *Primer Pintor de Cámara* ("First Painter to the Chamber", the highest rank among the royal painters), a post he was to hold until 1776; his portraits and frescoes in the Royal Palace were to make an enormous impression on Spanish painters. In 1762, Giambattista Tiepolo arrived in Madrid where, in spite of his sixty-six years, he executed the splendid frescoes of the Royal Palace and seven paintings for the church of San Pascual in Aranjuez. He was assisted by his sons Giandomenico and Lorenzo, who were to stay on in Spain after their father's death in 1770. The outstanding Spanish artists in Madrid at this time were Antonio González Ruiz, Luis Meléndez, the three González Velázquez brothers, Mariano Salvador Maella, Francisco Bayeu, José del Castillo and Luis Paret y Alcázar, who represent the transition from the last stages of the Baroque to the Academic.

In the minutes of the proceedings of the Royal Academy of San Fernando it is recorded that on 4th December 1763 Goya presented himself for examination for a student scholarship. The test consisted in drawing in pencil a *statue of Silenus*. Entrants for the competition had to complete the exercise by 15th January of the following year. The scholarship was awarded to Gregorio Ferro, a mediocre painter, who was to defeat Goya not only in this first encounter at the Academy but also on other occasions when they were both fully fledged artists. In January 1766, Goya again figures among the participants in a competition held by the Academy of San Fernando. Goya did not receive a single vote.

The journey to Italy for the purposes of study was an important step for a Spanish artist. It was, as we know, a first concern of the Spanish Academies to send young artists to Rome, and the "pensión" or travelling scholarship to Italy was the supreme reward for the most outstanding pupils. Goya's failures at the Academy, mentioned above, had deprived him of the advantage of undertaking a visit to Italy as a scholarship-holder, but he did not let this frustrate his desire, and in some way or other he made his way to Italy and worked in Rome. Goya himself was to declare later that the journey, of which we know neither the duration nor the itinerary, was undertaken at his own expense. In a letter written by Goya and dated in Rome on 20th April 1771, he informs the Royal Academy in Parma of the despatch of a painting submitted in the competition announced by the Parma Academy on 29th May 1770. Goya's painting of the subject set for the competition, *Hannibal Surveying Italy for the First Time from the Alps*, did not gain a prize but earned six votes and a favourable mention in the minutes of the results.

The material evidence of Goya's stay in Rome is confined to a few oil paintings on canvas: a portrait of *Manuel de Vargas Machuca*, an attractive painting that seems to anticipate in the smile of the sitter Goya's brilliant career as a portrait painter, and various scenes, Neo-Classical in feeling, in which he introduces types deriving from his previous works, but which more significantly foreshadow much in his later works, especially in his decorative paintings and his allegorical and imaginative compositions. These vigorous and assured paintings, full of grace and energy, constitute a really significant link in the chain of Goya's development. *Fig. 2*

About the middle of 1771, Goya was living in Zaragoza and working as an independent painter. This is confirmed by the official records of his taxes, paid to the town as an artisan. If one compares the sums contributed at this time, one finds that in less than three years Goya had succeeded in overtaking his own master Luzán and all the other artists of the Aragonese capital, demonstrating the intensity of his activity which enabled him to establish so rapidly a reputation and clientele.

He was awarded his first important commission on 21st October 1771, when the Chapter of the Basilica of El Pilar accepted his tender for the decoration of the vault of the choir in the Chapel of the Virgin, named in the documents the *Coreto*, or "little choir". On 11th November Goya submitted to the administrative board of the Basilica a painting in fresco as evidence of his proficiency in this technique. The contract was obtained in competition with Antonio González Velázques, who had been responsible for the decoration of the central dome, completed in 1753.

The year 1772 opened with Goya feverishly completing the preparatory study for the *Coreto* *Fig. 4* fresco, which he presented on 27th January to the Cathedral Board of Works, who judged it to be "a talented work of particular excellence" and decided to accept it, without first obtaining the approval of the Royal Academy in accordance with the procedure established by the Chapter in determining the terms of the contract. The study reveals how carefully Goya has considered all the details of the design, which he succeeds in bringing together with brilliant effect. The painting, depending especially on effects of light, places as much emphasis on the forms as on the free resolution of the painting problems, an approach which is confirmed in the *Vault fresco*, completed in June of the same year.

The remarkable *Self-Portrait* illustrates the painter's mastery at the age of about twenty-seven. *Fig. 5* A number of versions of the painting exist. It is the first of a series of self-portraits that continues throughout his career, recording truthfully and impassively the gradual transformation of his physiognomy. The portrait is charged with energy and indicates an early physical maturity. The occasion for this portrait was probably Goya's marriage to Francisco Bayeu's sister, Josefa. The marriage took place in Madrid on 25th July 1773. The young couple very soon left the capital, and Goya continued working in Zaragoza for more than another year.

This was a decisive year in the artist's life, both on account of the paintings for the Carthusian *Fig. 3* house of *Aula Dei* and because of the new step taken by Goya in moving to Madrid. The series of compositions, some ten feet high and painted in oils, that decorated like an enormous frieze the walls of the nave, crossing and choir of this Aragonese Carthusian foundation, were carried out between April and November of 1774. The technique which made it possible for him to complete the eleven large compositions in so short a time was his own discovery, based on his experience in fresco painting. Throughout his career Goya was frequently to make these skilful experiments with technique, handling one medium with the particular skill proper to another. The oil paintings of *Aula Dei* reveal his remarkable feeling for space and his talent for suggesting effects with the utmost economy of means. Only an intuitive genius of Goya's stature could have achieved these effects with so little elaboration of brushwork. These remarkable wall paintings, which constitute one of the outstanding masterpieces of Spanish painting of all time, close the first phase of Goya's career.

Works for the Tapestry Factory and introduction to the Court (1774-1785)

Goya probably arrived in Madrid at the end of 1774, having finally severed his connections with his native Aragon. According to his own declaration in a letter of 1779, he was called to the capital by Anton Raphael Mengs to take part in works for the Crown. His appointment to this new work must in fact have been made on the suggestion of Francisco Bayeu, who was one of the heads of the team of painters working for the Royal Tapestry Factory. What is known is that on their arrival in Madrid Goya and his wife were installed in the Bayeu house, situated in the Calle del Reloj. It was in this house that their first son was born, baptised on 15th December 1775, and it was here also that Goya began his new activity.

In 1775 Goya had commenced work as one of the painters engaged in the production of tapestry cartoons. We shall see that it was to be a long, hard struggle before he was to obtain the coveted official title of Pintor del Rey with a fixed salary and a permanent place among the established servants of the Crown. The painters of cartoons carried out their work in the workshops of the Santa Bárbara Factory, under the direction of Francesco Sabatini, the official architect-decorator of the royal residences. The tapestries were always made for specific destinations, for they were conceived as an integral part of the decoration of the walls of the palaces. The subjects were chosen by the King himself, or at least officially. At the time under discussion there was a predilection for popular genre scenes of a pronounced story-telling type.

Before starting on a cartoon the painter was required to submit for royal approval a preliminary sketch in oils, which remained the property of the artist. This was followed by drawings from life, executed in pencil or chalk on dark paper, of the individual figures to be included in the composition. The final work, executed in oils on a canvas primed with Sevillian ochre, followed exactly the original design.

Goya delivered his first cartoons on 24th May 1775. The compositions betray a stylistic indecision that can be attributed to a certain disorientation caused by his new environment and activity. A definite recovery is noticeable in the second delivery of cartoons, made on 30th October of the same year, which like the first represented hunting and fishing scenes. Goya learned increasingly to develop his painting within the limitations imposed.

There was an interruption of a few months in Goya's work for the Tapestry Factory. Since the modest income obtained from the two deliveries of cartoons in 1775 would hardly have allowed him to remain idle during this interruption — nor was idleness ever among his vices — we must suppose that he continued painting on his own account.

But the promise of regular work offered by working officially for the Royal Factory was a great temptation. Thus, at some time in 1776, Goya, Ramón Bayeu and José del Castillo applied for official appointments as painters to the Royal Tapestry Factory. The application of the three painters was turned down, but it was not long before they resumed their work for the Royal Factory, on the basis of payment for the works alone according to their valuation.

1777 was a year that saw Goya's growing confidence and sense of security confirmed. In a letter to Zapater he declares that, though still convalescing from a serious illness, he is painting "with greater acceptance", which indicates an adaptation, however temporary, to the demands and restrictions of the particular circumstances. The year was, in fact, one especially devoted to *Figs. 7 and 8-9* the painting of tapestry cartoons. On 3rd March he delivered his *Dance on the Banks of the Manzanares*, the pair to *The Picnic*, finished in October of 1776. On 12th August he delivered four *Fig. 6* cartoons and on 25th January of the following year a further four cartoons. These cartoons, which *Figs. 10-11* include works of such high attainment as *The Parasol*, certainly one of the most popular paintings in Spanish art, which was to make so widespread an impression, demonstrate Goya's ability in the face of artistic concepts and conditions that must have incited his innate nonconformity. The sketch *Figs. 12 and 13-14* for *The Fight at the New Inn*, the only sketch extant connected with the cartoons produced in this year, is sufficient to show the remarkable skill of these preparatory studies.

In the first months of the year 1778 he only produced one cartoon, *The Blind Man with the Guitar*, delivered in April. The painting is of complex structure, with fine nuances of tone. It is not surprising that the director of the Tapestry Factory should have complained, on receiving the cartoon, of the pictorial effects of the cartoons provided by Goya, on account of the difficulty of reproducing them in the tapestries, "more especially the shimmer of his changing tones..., which takes so much time and patience". The satisfactory transfer of a cartoon to tapestry does in fact demand a comparative simplicity of treatment in the cartoon, as much in the forms as in the colour scheme and general treatment. Hence the decorative effect of many of Goya's cartoons; on other occasions, however, he would exceed the normal demands of the cartoon and essay an inspired and vital autonomous painting. In the case of *The Blind Man with the Guitar*, however, Goya found himself obliged to modify his cartoon. His first design is possibly recorded in his etching of the same subject, which shows distinct differences from the final cartoon. In a letter to Zapater in 1778, with which he sends his friend a sketch for the *Dance on the Banks of the Manzanares*, Goya tells of Sabatini, the Architect and Director of Works for the Crown, visiting him in his studio and taking away a number of his beautiful sketches, "leaving me naked". In the same letter he tells Zapater he has sent him "a series of engravings after paintings in the Royal Palace". This refers to the series of etchings after Velázquez's works. In themselves the engravings do not add much to Goya's reputation, for copying was never his forte and he was always most successful when working freely and independently, but the undertaking was important in leading him to a deep study of Spain's great seventeenth-century painter. Goya was able to appreciate the pictorial value of Velázquez's reflected lights, of which that master was the supreme exponent, and he applied them in painting his tapestry cartoons and later his portraits. In his sketches, too, we find Goya introducing Velázquez's long brushstrokes, with their density of colour and immediate and precise definition of form.

On 5th January of the year 1779, Goya delivered a series of six original cartoons. In appraising the paintings Maella declared that they were "very well painted". On this occasion Goya took part for the first time in the presentation of works for royal approval. He describes the event in a letter to Zapater, which is worth quoting for its real human interest: "If I had the leisure I would tell you how the King and the Prince and Princess honoured me, graciously giving me leave to show them four paintings and kiss their hands, which is the very first time that anything like this has happened; and I can tell you that I could not wish more of their reception of my works and of the satisfaction they showed in seeing them, and of the graciousness shown to me by the king and even more by their Highnesses. And afterwards, God be thanked, by all the Court, and it is more that I or my works warrant." It is not surprising that the paintings pleased the royal family, for they include some of the finest of his cartoons, such as, for instance, that feast of colour, *The Crockery Vendor*. Goya had in these works succeeded in completely mastering the potentialities of this charming narrative and decorative genre, transforming it into a delightful display of virtuosity and of his inexhaustible inventiveness in composition. The series may properly be seen as one of the final triumphs of the Rococo style, which Goya was soon to replace by a more dramatic art, in sympathy with his more profound nature. In the letter quoted above we have seen with what pleasure he received the first signs of royal favour, and this was important to him, for he had now begun to incur envy. "I am beginning", he says in the same letter, "to have more enemies, and more malicious ones".

Figs. 15-16

In June of this year Anton Raphael Mengs had died in Rome, leaving a vacant place among the *Painters to the Chamber*, for which Goya took the opportunity to apply. It was in this application that he made the statement, already mentioned, that he had undertaken a journey to Rome at his own expense. His application was not successful, but in the report on the candidates he was adjudged "a talented and industrious master who promises considerable progress in his art".

In the course of 1779 he probably painted thirteen cartoons altogether, two delivered on 20th July and the remaining eleven on 24th January of the following year, all of them intended to decorate the antechamber to the bedrooms of the Prince and Princess of Asturias, in the Pardo Palace. The most outstanding among them is *The Washerwomen*, in which the rendering of the distances anticipates certain works of his final phase. This delivery of cartoons closed the first period of activity for the Royal Tapestry Factory, for on account of the war with England the Crown stopped for the time being all expenditure on items of luxury and art.

Figs. 17 to 19

Figs. 20-21

Goya receives his first official recognition, election to membership of the Royal Academy of San Fernando, which no doubt reflected the views of his brother-in-law, Francisco Bayeu. In his application of 5th May he declares himself a pupil of that royal establishment. As his diploma piece, demanded by the rules of the corporation, he submitted on 7th May a life-size *Christ Crucified*. This really remarkable work has not always received unqualified admiration, probably because it has invited comparison with Velázquez's famous *Christ*. If the painting does fall short of a supreme achievement, this is probably less because the subject was not the most congenial to Goya than because in his desire to produce a strictly academic painting he employed one of Bayeu's designs, which in turn was based on one of Mengs' paintings. Nevertheless, Goya surpassed both his models by a long way. To this period must belong the remarkable portrait Goya painted of his brother-in-law, doubtless in recognition of the latter's efforts on his behalf.

Fig. 22

Fig. 23

On Goya's returning to Zaragoza for some time, there began a series of events which were to have a profound effect on his outlook. At a meeting of the Board of Works of the Basilica of El Pilar on 23rd May 1780, it was decided to give Goya the commission to paint one of the cupolas of the great church, with its respective pendentives. The commission was given to him on the instigation of Francisco Bayeu, who had been appointed inspector of the decorations of the church. The fee of three thousand *pesos* (45,000 *reales*) was a modest one, but Goya accepted the commission with enthusiasm and gratification. He writes to Zapater asking him to find lodgings for himself and his wife: "I do not need much furniture for my house, and I think with a print of Our Lady of the Pillar, a table, five chairs, a frying-pan, a wine bottle, a guitar, a roasting-jack and a lamp, anything else would be superfluous." Goya was not able to undertake the journey to Zaragoza until the autumn, after the birth of a son who died soon afterwards. On 5th October he presented the sketches to the Chapter, which accepted them, and he immediately started work on the fresco.

Very soon he came into conflict with his brother-in-law, Bayeu, who disagreed with Goya's pictorial approach and his method of painting the enormous fresco. The experienced Academician had at this moment reached a point of perfection in his particular style, honest and correct, but lacking in genius. Away from Madrid, Goya again felt himself free and ready to repeat with greater experience and increased assurance his early great — though little-known — achievements of the *Coreto* and Aula Dei. A clash between the forces of the established order and his developing genius was inevitable, and it was equally inevitable that the forces of the established order were to prevail; and so the Zaragoza enterprise, undertaken with so much promise, was to become a small drama that would leave Goya embittered for many years.

At a meeting of the Board on 14th December, the administrator of the prebendary council, Don Matías Allué, reported to the Chapter Francisco Bayeu's report of Goya's refusal to take notice of his recommendations, and his consequent request to be excused from his responsibility as director of the work as far as it concerned his brother-in-law. It was decided that Allué should speak to Goya and draw his attention to such defects in the painting as had been noticed. The painter paid no heed and continued with his painting until it was finished, probably at the end of January 1781.

It is true that Goya did introduce certain technical innovations in his painting, and also certain distortions, in consideration of the optical problems. And he certainly gave way to his urge to stress the expressive effects of the painting, apparent in certain passages of colour and complexities of line that put any measured academic handling out of the question. In addition to the experience he had gained and the development of his painting in the course of his work on the tapestry cartoons in Madrid, Goya had also begun to regain his personality, and he was unable to look back. It was inevitable that he should finally declare his aesthetic approach and insist on the freedom of his method. When one looks today at the effect of the whole decoration, it is difficult to appreciate *Figs. 24 to 27* Bayeu's disapproval, for the cupola of the *Regina Martyrum* seems a work of exalted idealism, noble in its composition and harmonious in its colour and tone; a work that perfectly reflects the transition between Baroque and Neo-Classicism. When one looks more closely, however, at the figures and the details, full of bold and energetic improvisation, one is also aware of its Romantic spirit.

On 11th February 1781 there was a further meeting of the Board, when it was announced that Goya had completed the painting of the cupola and that he should now submit the sketches for the decoration of the pendentives, which were to represent allegories of Faith, Fortitude, Charity and Patience. Goya's sketches were examined by the Board on 10th March and rejected, the Chapter declaring that in its judgement, which no doubt reflected Bayeu's views, Charity was portrayed with scant decorum and the other virtues were meagre and obscure. At the same meeting it was decided that Goya should be instructed to prepare new sketches and also place himself under the direction of his brother-in-law for the purpose of retouching the painting of the cupola. Goya's reply, respectful but firm, appears in a lengthy memorial he prepared, probably with the assistance of his loyal and equable friend Zapater, part of which is quoted for the light it sheds on the artist's personality: his "attention has been drawn to the opinions expressed, which would seem to be informed by considerations other than that of justice, or at least not by considerations of the rules governing art... an artist's professional honour is a very delicate thing, and upon his reputation depends his whole livelihood..."; and for this reason he wished to defend himself. He declares that he had accepted the commission on the understanding that he was to be given complete freedom in its execution: "The qualification of being an elected member of the Academy of San Fernando" and the works he had produced "do not allow me, without prejudice to my honour, to submit to absolute dependence on another master". He declares that he had willingly submitted the sketches to Bayeu for his approval, "and I have done nothing in carrying them out but transform the small paintings into large-scale ones".

He asks finally that his work be judged by the Academicians Mariano Maella and Antonio González Velázquez. Thereupon, Fray Félix Salcedo, a Carthusian brother from Aula Dei, intervened as mediator, and in a letter to Goya dated 30th March declared that, "the affair with Don Francisco Bayeu" having come to his knowledge, he recommends humility, and that Goya accept the decision of the Board of Works and the judgement of his brother-in-law, "for if the work is good, judgement will advertise it as such to all... and the work will be such that it will always bear witness to your merit".

Goya accepted Salcedo's arguments, and in a letter of 6th April addressed to Canon Allué he expressed his readiness to make fresh designs for the pendentives and to retouch the frescoes of the cupola according to his brother-in-law's suggestions. The new sketches were submitted on 17th April and approved by the Council and Bayeu, and in May the frescoes were finished. Before Goya returned to Madrid, however, there were further disagreements with the Chapter, the outcome of which was that the Chapter recorded its decision "that on no account and in no manner should Goya be allowed to do any more work for the church", and this decision was adhered to.

Back again in Madrid, it was not long before Goya received an important commission from the Crown; in a letter dated 25th July 1781 he tells Martin Zapater that he has received an offer from the King to paint a large canvas as one of the seven altarpieces for the church of San Francisco el Grande. The commissions for the six other paintings were simply given to the most eminent painters in Madrid: Francisco Bayeu, Andrés de la Calleja, José del Castillo, Gregorio Ferro, Mariano Salvador Maella and Antonio González Velázquez.

It would seem that the choice of Goya as one of the painters for San Francisco el Grande was due to the good offices of the Aragonese nobleman Juan Martín Goicoechea, a friend of the Chief Minister, the Conde de Floridablanca. On 22nd September, Goya notified the Minister of the subject *Fig. 28* he had chosen for his painting: *The Preaching of Saint Bernardino of Siena Before Alfonso V of Aragon*.

In January 1783 the paintings of San Francisco el Grande were in their places awaiting examination and final approval, which took place in November of the following year. First there was a period of spiritual dissatisfaction in Goya's life, in an atmosphere of expectations and disappointments. His bitterness is expressed in a rather confused letter of 22nd January: "If I were able to tell you everything that may be known in time, all these irritations might end; but since it is in other hands and does not depend on me, it does not matter; and so my horse will come in when I see it."

The first breath of hope came from the Chief Minister, José Moñino, Conde de Floridablanca, *Fig. 33* who honoured him by allowing him to paint his portrait. This painting, an elaborately worked-out composition which introduced strokes of genius and new ideas, and at the same time posed problems which Goya was not yet ready to solve, was received with a certain coldness by the all-powerful statesman. The hurt inflicted by this unsuccessful outcome of the painting was still felt a year later: "My friend, there is nothing new and there is still the same silence in my affair with Señor Moñino as before I made the portrait. The most he has said to me is, 'Goya, we will see later'." "Everyone is surprised that it should have come to nothing with the Minister of State after having given him so much satisfaction; and if nothing does come from this, there is no need to hope any more; and being kept waiting so long for what one has only deserved, one only despairs the more". We may infer from this that the portrait brought Goya neither material nor moral reward.

In Goya's time it was indeed only possible for an artist to succeed in his career by the slow and gradual process of gaining access to the circles of the well-to-do, and then — and this was more essential — obtaining some official appointment or benefice that would open up doors otherwise closed. Thus an artist could ignore no opportunity of advancing his position. To have friends and patrons was very important, and Goya realized this. It was Ventura Rodríguez, the architect of El Pilar, who probably helped to open to Goya the doors of the Palace of the Infante Luis de Borbón, the King's brother. This Infante was living away from the Court on account of his morganatic marriage to an Aragonese lady, Maria Teresa Vallabriga, after being obliged to renounce his Cardinal's biretta and the Archbishopric of Toledo. In August and September of 1783 Goya spent four weeks at the Infante's country residence at Arenas de San Pedro, in the province of Avila. The painter more than repaid this hospitality by his intense activity. In the four weeks of his stay at Arenas, Goya painted from life the studies for the heads of Don Luis and his wife, and the larger portraits of the Infante's wife and of the two children of the marriage, Luis, the future Cardinal *Figs. 29 to 32* of Toledo, who was later to hold the Regency of the Kingdom during one of Spain's most tragic times, and Maria Teresa, the future Condesa de Chinchón and wife of Godoy.

To judge from a letter to Zapater dated 20th September 1783, Goya returned from his brief stay in Luis de Borbón's little court contented and optimistic, in spite of the fact that his material gain from the visit was no more than a few *reales* and the gift of a dress "all in gold and silver" for his wife, which the Infante's steward told him was worth thirty thousand *reales* — and Goya was credulous enough to believe it!

Through the good offices of the statesman Gaspar Melchor de Jovellanos, Goya was given a commission to paint four large canvases for the Calatrava College of Salamanca University. In the letter to Goya informing him of the order to pay the four hundred doubloons in payment for the work already finished, the statesman says: "I am satisfied with the care and application with which you have carried out the paintings and with their outstanding merit." Unfortunately the paintings, representing *Saints Bernard, Benedict and Raimundo* and *The Immaculate Conception*, were destroyed during the Napoleonic Wars, the only one to have survived being the preparatory sketch for the last-named. It would seem likely that he painted the splendid portrait of the Minister *Fig. 34* himself at this time, but since it falls in line with Goya's great series of portraits it may have been painted somewhat later than 1784.

Goya continued to have hopes of the outcome of his work for the church of San Francisco el Grande. He refers to it in a letter of 31st October: "The King has just ordered that the church of San Francisco be made ready, for it appears that he intends to celebrate there the ceremony of the Orders. I am putting the last touches to my painting, of which you will hear, as of the others, for it is an occasion much looked forward to by the artists and the *dilettanti* alike. The other painters are doing the same, except my brother-in-law, who says that he will be coming from Toledo at the end of the month and that his painting requires no retouching." The paintings of San Francisco remained covered until November 1784. Goya's great hopes then dissolved like a mirage. The brief comment with which Floridablanca closed the case is self-explanatory: "The paintings are nothing of great importance, except that those by Goya, Ferro and Castillo are the least bad." On 2nd December of this year another son, Francisco Javier, was born to the painter, the only one to survive him.

In 1785 Goya's situation seems to become clearer. Apparently on the initiative of Agustín Ceán Bermúdez, the famous Spanish art historian and a good friend of Goya's, the painter was commissioned to paint a series of portraits for the Board of Directors of the Bank of San Carlos. The first was that of José Toro y Zambrano, for which he received 2,328 *reales* on 13th April 1785.

On 17th May Goya was appointed Deputy Director of Painting at the Academy of San Fernando, which involved an appreciable amount of work and brought in the modest remuneration of twenty doubloons annually. He occupied the place left vacant by Andrés de la Calleja, a painter deserving more notice, whose technique, freer than that of Bayeu, possibly exercised some influence on the young Goya. The artist gained other patrons in this year; some, like the Dukes of Medinaceli and Osuna, were to continue their friendship and patronage for a large part of Goya's career. From the Duke of Medinaceli he received the commission to paint a large *Annunciation* for the Capuchin church of San Antonio del Prado in Madrid. The painting still exists, and also the beautiful preliminary sketch, which illustrates the progress made by Goya in the direction of simplification.

Fig. 35
He also made two oil paintings of the *Duke and Duchess of Osuna*, which were paid for on 16th July. The beautiful quality of the portrait of the Duchess, with the rich harmony of its colours, could deservedly take its place among the most outstanding of Goya's female portraits, which as a series constitute one of the artist's finest achievements. It seems in this case that the Duchess's captivating personality, clearly described in contemporary accounts, succeeded in breaking down the barrier of inhibitions that seem to have hampered the painter's natural spontaneity when confronted with sitters of high station.

Royal Painter and Painter to the Chamber (1786-1792)

In a letter dated 11th March 1786, Goya confides to his friend in Zaragoza the state of his growing balance of shares held in the Bank of San Carlos, the interest on which, together with his salary from the Academy and the moneys outstanding from commissions, amounted to an annual income of some twelve to thirteen thousand *reales*. This was not much, but in his letter he declares: "And withal I am as content as the most fortunate."

Cornelius Van der Gotten, the Director of the Royal Tapestry Factory, died on 25th March 1786, and his nephew, Livinio Stuyck, applied for the vacant post. For their part, however, the royal painters Bayeu and Maella addressed a memorandum to the Minister, Floridablanca, recommending that the directorship of the Royal Factory should be in the hands of Spanish artists; at the same time they proposed that two painters should be appointed for the express purpose of working on the cartoons, and with a salary that would allow them to devote themselves completely to this work.

The Royal decision was made public on 25th June: Stuyck was to assume the Directorship, and Ramón Bayeu and Goya, proposed respectively by the former's brother and by Maella, were appointed *Pintores del Rey*, each with an annual salary of fifteen thousand *reales*. The requirement to devote himself exclusively to his new task was to remain a dead letter as far as Goya was concerned.

Goya's acceptance of his new appointment, which he jubilantly communicated to Zapater, was to have the effect of immediately doubling his income. Thus the artist had finally secured a comfortable and steady income. There can be no doubt that this had an important bearing on the very evident change effected in his subsequent works, both in his approach and in his method. He was not ambitious in the ordinary sense, but he needed the material security to allay his anxiety and attain peace of mind.

Figs. 38 to 42
In October he presented to the King, who was residing in the Escorial at the time, the sketches for the tapestries for the dining-hall of the Palace of El Pardo. These comprised: *Flower-Sellers, The Threshing-Ground, The Grape-Harvest, The Snowstorm, Poor People at the Fountain, The Drunken Mason* (which for reasons of propriety became *The Wounded Mason* in the final version of the cartoon), *The Boy on the Ram, Two Children with Two Mastiffs, Hunter Beside a Fountain* and *Shepherd Playing the Flageolet*. Some of these preliminary sketches still exist, and they are among the gayest of all Goya's designs for tapestries, just as the corresponding cartoons are among the finest paintings he did for the Royal Factory. He began painting the cartoons at the beginning of the following year, for in a report dated 20th December, Goya and Ramón Bayeu informed Francesco Sabatini that they were unable to pay in advance for the canvases, stretchers and colours for the royal works, and in addition the daily payment of six reales each to a colour-grinder, required by each of them. An order was accordingly issued to meet these expenditures, but to include one colour-grinder only to serve both painters.

Figs. 36-37
At this moment of optimism Goya forgot old grievances and painted the remarkable portrait of *Francisco Bayeu*, a work which heralds the beginning of his maturity. One is aware immediately of the enormous distance which separates this portrait in grey and black from the portraits of polite society of the preceding years. He also painted in this year, for the Bank of San Carlos, the portraits of the *Marqués de Tolosa*, the *Conde de Altamira* and *Carlos III* in court dress. For the three portraits he received ten thousand *reales* in January 1787. In April he delivered to the Duke and Duchess of Osuna eight paintings made for the Alameda, the Duke's sumptuous country residence. They are very large oil paintings, of an exquisite grace appropriate to their essentially decorative purpose, and call to mind the spirit of the tapestry cartoons. For these works and another small painting representing "the portraits of the three children in full-length", he received twenty-two thousand *reales*. In October 1787 three large paintings still preserved in the church of the monastery of Santa

Ana in Valladolid were presented to the public. On the fifteenth of that month Goya was paid by the Bank of San Carlos for a new portrait: that of *Francisco Larrumbe.*

In 1788 Goya received a commission from the Conde de Altamira to paint the portraits of his wife and of his son Manuel. Goya also painted in this year the portrait of the *Conde de Cabarrús,* the last one for the portrait gallery of the Bank of San Carlos. On 31st May he writes to his friend Zapater announcing that he is preparing the designs for the tapestry cartoons to adorn the bedroom of the Infantas in the Palace of El Pardo, which are to be ready in time "for their arrival at the Court, and on which I am working with much perseverance and anxiety, for there is very little time, and the King, Princes, etc. have to see them; and on top of this the subjects are difficult and involve a lot of work, like *The Meadow of San Isidro* on the Saint's feast-day, which has to be shown with all the activity usual on this occasion at this place. I tell you truthfully as a friend that I am beside myself and can neither sleep nor rest until the thing is finished, and you cannot call this living as I live..."

From this letter to Zapater and from documents in the Royal Archives it can be deduced that Goya painted in 1788 four preliminary oil sketches for cartoons for *The Meadow of San Isidro, The Hermitage of San Isidro, The Picnic* and *Blind-man's-buff,* of which he only painted the cartoon for the last-mentioned, which was delivered in the early months of 1789.

In June Goya applied for the post of Director of Painting at the Academy. It is almost unbelievable, but all his fellow Academicians voted against him. The post was filled by the mediocre painter Gregorio Ferro, who a long time before, in 1766, had defeated Goya in the Academy competition. On 2nd July Goya writes: "I am very grieved that I have not carried out your order, since it is for you, but the same has happened with the Archbishop of Toledo, who has given me a commission for a painting for his church, and I have not even been able to make a sketch for it. You will see that I cannot help it, for I want to satisfy everyone, they only have to remember me, but I am wishing now they did not remember me but allowed me to live in peace and do those works which I have promised to do, and give the rest of the time to things that I want to do and am unable to."

On 16th October 1788 he was paid by the Duke and Duchess of Osuna for the two large paintings which decorate the Chapel of Saint Francis of Borja in Valencia Cathedral. Stylistically they would seem to be veritable products of the Romantic Age, or of nineteenth-century historical painting. One must admit, before these paintings, that Goya himself seems to have been somewhat confused by the extravagant requirements of the narrative. But even in works unsympathetic to his genius there are always passages of originality.

On this same date he was paid for the portrait of *The Duke and Duchess of Osuna with their children.* In this work the painter submerges his sitters in a greyish, luminous, pre-Impressionist haze, out of which the eyes of the two parents and the four children emerge, lending an almost obsessive character to their look. The delicacy of execution and the harmony of the forms, tone and space in this intimate family portrait are a remarkable achievement. For this portrait he received twelve thousand *reales* in February 1789.

On 14th December 1788, Carlos III died. He was succeeded by his son Carlos, who had married María Luisa of Parma, and the proclamation of the new King took place on 17th January 1789. The late King, a good and diligent ruler, had never succeeded in appreciating Goya's art. On the other hand, the new King, Carlos IV, seems to have felt a definite admiration for the artist's work from the time he was Prince of Asturias, and after his coronation he was not long in conferring on the painter the coveted title of Painter to the Chamber *(Pintor de Cámara).* Goya was sworn in to his new post — which brought with it no increase in the modest stipend he received as Painter to the King in the service of the Royal Tapestry Factory — in Aranjuez on 30th April. One can visualize him occupied in the laborious task of painting the portraits of the new royal family, in which all the official royal painters and their assistants were engaged, and which started even before Goya's new appointment.

On 20th February 1790, Goya writes to Zapater that he has just finished and delivered personally a painting commissioned by Carlos IV for his brother, the King of Naples. He says that the King expressed his satisfaction verbally, "putting his hands on my shoulders and half-embracing me and abusing the Aragonese and the Zaragozans". It has not been possible to identify the painting in question. In the same letter he complains about his family, and especially about his brothers, who were gradually trying to get more and more out of him. He explains that what he spends on himself is necessary, now that he is so well-known and has to keep up a way of living consonant with his status, but at the same time he indicates that his new way of living is as he would like it.

It is at this time that he must have painted the picture representing the *Visit of the Virgin to Saint Julian,* for the side of the High Altar of the parish church of Valdemoro. The fact that Francisco Bayeu painted the central composition for the same High Altar, which he dated and signed in 1790, and his brother Ramón Bayeu painted the pair to Goya's panel, indicates that the harmonious relationship between the families continued.

In 1791 Goya was probably much engaged on private commissions and endeavouring to avoid as far as possible his work for the Crown. In May of this year he painted the portrait of the boy *Luis María de Cistué,* another addition to his splendid series of child portraits. It is interesting to note how different is his portrayal of children in his portraits from that of his tapestry cartoons.

Fig. 43

Figs. 44-45

Fig. 46

Figs. 47-48

Fig. 49

The former are of children of aristocratic birth; the latter, children of the people, mischievous and unkempt; and he adapts his style brilliantly to these distinct tasks.

He continued to assist in the preparation of the inventories and the valuation of the paintings of the Royal Palaces, which was completed on 23rd August of this year. He may well have considered that this task was sufficient, since the post of Painter to the King did not bring with it any increase of salary. When he was urged to paint some cartoons, the measurements for which had been given to him some years before, he put off the work with legalistic excuses that provoked angry reactions from Sabatini and the directors of the Royal Tapestry Factory. On 13th April the Director of the Factory, Stuyck, addressed a memorandum to the King declaring that there was no work for the tapestry makers since no cartoons were forthcoming from the official Court painters, Goya and Ramón Bayeu. The royal command in reply was immediate and unequivocal: "That Goya be told to do these designs." It seems that the event was occasioned by some petty intrigue among the members of the royal household.

In response to the royal command, Goya began painting the preliminary studies for the cartoons for the tapestries, intended for the decoration of the King's study in the Escorial. In an undated letter, which according to Sambricio was probably written at the end of December 1791, Goya tells Zapater of his visit to the King, who received him "with great pleasure... and shook my hand, and began to play the violin...". The painter adds that it was with some apprehension that he visited the King, since some colleague had told the latter that Goya had no desire to serve him. It would seem probable that this incident took place on the occasion of Goya's presentation to the King of the preliminary sketches for the cartoons. Goya did not omit to pay his visit to Zaragoza this year, for which he was granted leave on 4th October. He apparently only stayed some three weeks in the Aragonese capital, for on 6th November he attended a meeting of the Academy in Madrid.

Figs. 50-51

The first half of 1792 must have been devoted to the execution of the cartoons after the preliminary sketches made in the previous year. He probably painted then some portraits of the King and Queen, wearing the sashes of the Order of Carlos III in the new form of this decoration introduced in 1792.

Thanks to the decision taken by the Academy of San Fernando — on 1st July 1792 — to appoint a commission to decide upon the reform of its teaching programme, we are acquainted with Goya's opinion on such matters, for in his minutes of the meeting Isidoro Bosarte transcribes it as follows: "Señor Goya declares himself openly for freedom in the teaching and practice of the styles, rejecting the servile discipline of children's schools, mechanical rules, the monthly prizes, monetary assistance and other trifling things that only enfeeble and debase painting. Nor should time be given up to the teaching of geometry and perspective in order to overcome the difficulties of drawing."

Deafness and intense creative activity.
First Painter to the Chamber (1792-1806)

The painter fell ill in Seville at the end of December 1792. According to Sánchez Cantón, it was probably Ceán Bermúdez who took him to the Cadiz house of the collector and bibliophile Sebastián Martínez, who, being aware of Goya's difficult position, since the artist had made the journey to Andalusia without the King's leave, arranged with Bayeu to apply for the leave of absence on Goya's behalf, acting as if the artist had fallen ill in Madrid.

On 19th March 1793, Martínez writes to a palace functionary, Pedro Arascot, requesting an extension of leave for Goya, "who is still unable to write owing to the disturbance in his head, which is where all his sickness affects him". He explains that "Goya left the court, as your honour is aware, with the intention of seeing this city and those on the way here, in doing which he spent the two months' leave granted to him, but he unfortunately fell ill in Seville and, believing that he would be better looked after here [Cadiz], he decided to come here, accompanied by a friend, and he entered my house in the truly pitiable state in which he is still, being unable to leave the house".

A letter from Martínez to Zapater, dated 29th March, gives news of the artist: "Goya continues to be very weak although he has improved a little", and "the noise in his head and the deafness have not stopped". On 30th March, Zapater writes to Bayeu to thank him for succeeding in obtaining the grant of leave for Goya, whom he blames for thoughtlessness in undertaking the journey.

Much has been written about the nature of this illness, and the various opinions of eminent specialists, generally contradictory, have not succeeded in solving the problem. It is clear that the illness was of a very serious nature, that the convalescence was very prolonged and that it left Goya completely deaf for the remaining forty years of his life. This fact inevitably had an effect on his character and forced his life into a new pattern. It did not, however, lead to any relaxation of Goya's tireless activity, but seems rather to have encouraged an even more intense activity and to have accentuated the artist's inclination to delve into the dark and fantastic.

It is not known when Goya returned to Madrid. On 11th July 1793 he attended a meeting of the Academy of San Fernando, and it is therefore possible that he had started to paint again at

17

this time, while still convalescing, taking his first steps in his new world of isolation. We have testimony of this in the well-known letter of 4th January 1794, addressed to Bernardo de Iriarte, in which he declares: "To occupy my mind, afflicted by my illness, and to defray in part the great expenses that it has brought about, I have devoted myself to painting a series of studio pictures in which I have succeeded in making observations usually impossible to make in commissioned works, which give no scope to the imagination and invention. I have thought fit to offer them to the Academy for whatever purpose you may think fit." Eleven paintings in all, of "popular diversions", were presented to the Academy, where they were praised for "their own merit and that of Goya". In a letter of 7th January 1794, the painter expressed his appreciation to Iriarte and the Academy for their kind words, and added that to complete the series he was painting a "Madhouse scene, with two men fighting naked, and the warden beating them, and others in sacks", to which he adds "It is a scene I witnessed in Zaragoza". *Fig. 53*

Fig. 52

Everything seems to indicate that Goya was again enjoying good health in the year 1795 and that he had resigned himself, or at least adapted himself, to his deafness. He had learned to speak in sign language with his hands. In the Instituto de Valencia de Don Juan in Madrid there is a drawing showing these signs, which according to an inscription at the foot of the drawing was done by Goya himself.

It is very likely that he painted in this year the pictures for the *Santa Cueva* in Cadiz, which are among the finest of his religious paintings. A panel in this church painted by Zacarías González Velázquez is dated in 1795. The church was consecrated on 31st March 1796. Goya probably executed his three large paintings in Madrid.

At the meeting of the Academy on 13th September, Goya was elected Director of Painting as successor to Francisco Bayeu, finally defeating his constant rival, Gregorio Ferro. It seems that he presented himself for election only to have the satisfaction of gaining the victory, since a few months later he presented his resignation, whereupon he was appointed Honorary Director by the Academicians in recognition of his merits.

It is in this year 1795 that the name of the Duchess of Alba first appears in Goya's life. We shall not dwell on this lady's well-known and over-popularized personality. We agree with the view so expertly presented by Sánchez Cantón in his *Vida y obras de Goya*. He sums up the problem as follows: "There are sufficient indications to allow one to conclude that Goya was enamoured of the Duchess of Alba, but not enough to affirm that his feelings were reciprocated." But although the story is somewhat outside the scope of the present book, the really important facts will be cited in their appropriate place. For the moment we quote the first documentary evidence, the famous paragraph in a letter from the artist to Zapater: "It would be more worth your while to come and help me paint the [Duchess of] Alba, who came to my studio for me to paint her face, which was done; and it is certainly more to my liking than painting her picture, which I also have to paint in full-length, and it will be done as soon as I have finished a sketch I am making of the Duke of Alcudia [Godoy] on horseback." *Fig. 54*

On 9th June 1796 the Duke of Alba died in Seville and the Duchess spent her period of mourning on her country estate at Sanlúcar de Barrameda, in the province of Seville. Various evidence indicates that Goya made a prolonged stay there at this time. There are also two albums of drawings connected with this stay on the Alba estate. They certainly contain some sketches of the Duchess and various members of her little country court. Some of these sketches were to be basic elements for the composition of the *Caprichos*. It was, in fact, just after this stay at Sanlúcar that Goya began to work actively on this series of etchings, which was finally published in 1799.

In 1797 is dated the famous portrait of *The Duchess of Alba* dressed in black, the most persuasive testimony of the painter's passionate interest in her. The two eloquent rings worn by the lady, inscribed with the names of Alba and Goya respectively, have now been joined by another piece of incontestable evidence, discovered in a recent cleaning of the canvas. An inscription traced in the sand, to which the Duchess is pointing with her hand, reads: "Sólo Goya" (Only Goya). But in deference to truth we must also admit that there is some contrary evidence. The indiscreet "Sólo" that precedes Goya's name was covered with a layer of paint almost contemporary with the original pigment of the canvas. Did Goya perhaps add such a compromising signature in the obsessive solitude of his studio? It seems, moreover, that the painting never left Goya's possession, since it is listed in the inventory of his effects made after the death of his wife in 1812 for the purpose of apportioning the estate between him and his son. The portrait of the Duchess then became the property of Javier Goya, probably with the signature modified. Further evidence of the artist's feelings for the Duchess is the etching entitled *Dream of Lying and Inconstancy*. This, in effect, is a confession of failure, for it shows Goya asleep and the Duchess with two faces and butterfly wings, that is, dissembling and rejecting. This engraving, of the same type and size as other plates of the *Caprichos*, was not included in the definitive series published in 1799, presumably because of the directness of the allusion. *Fig. 55*

In 1798 Goya renewed his acquaintance with the Duke and Duchess of Osuna, who bought six of his paintings of witchcraft scenes for the decoration of their country seat, "La Alameda", where so many of the great painter's works were assembled. Most probably these paintings were not specially commissioned. *Fig. 56*

The physical aspect of the splendid portrait of *The bullfighter Pedro Romero* causes us to attribute it to the period between 1796 and 1798. It is a living portrait, a veritable miracle of simplicity *Fig. 57* achieved with brushwork that is fleeting but restrained. There is also a replica of this portrait which we consider to have been painted by Goya himself, as well as various copies. All of this is natural, bearing in mind the great fame won in all the rings of Spain by the Andalusian matador, who was a great friend of Goya's.

Fig. 58

Another important milestone in the history of bullfighting, and in that of Goya himself, is the *Fighting bull* painted on canvas, which, in its expressiveness and the magic of its colouring, should obviously be classified with the portrait of Romero, both chronologically and technically.

Painted in 1798, almost certainly in the first half of that year, were the following portraits: that of *Andrés Peral*, which was shown in the Academy's summer exhibition, that of the embroiderer *Juan López* and that of the Valencian painter *Ascensió Juliá*, who was to be Goya's assistant in the work done in San Antonio de la Florida.

Figs. 59 to 62

On 22nd March of this year, taking advantage of the fact that Jovellanos was Minister for Justice and Saavedra Minister for Finance, Goya petitioned the former for payment of arrears of salary as a *Pintor del Rey*, alleging that it was his attacks of illness that had prevented him from working for the Crown for five years. He adds: "Your assistance is absolutely indispensable for such work as His Majesty may deign to entrust to me." It was almost certainly Jovellanos who then obtained for him one of the most important commissions of his career: the decoration of the hermitage of *San Antonio de la Florida*, a royal possession near Madrid. We may recall that in 1784 Jovellanos had already got him a commission for some paintings for Salamanca. On the present occasion the artist painted another portrait of the statesman. A proof of the integrity of Jovellanos, who never accepted gifts and sincerely desired to help his friend Goya, is that he paid Goya six thousand *reales* for the portrait. Unfortunately for Spain, the great statesman was soon to relinquish his post in the government. The following letter from Goya to Zapater probably refers to Jovellanos: "The day before yesterday I arrived at Aranjuez and for that reason have not replied to you. The minister has exceeded himself in his hospitality, taking me for a drive in his coach and treating me with the greatest possible friendliness; he allowed me to wear my cloak at table because it was so cold and has learnt to talk with his hands, interrupting his eating to talk to me. He wanted me to stay until Easter and to paint a portrait of Saavedra (who is a friend of his), and I should very much have liked to do so, but I had no canvases and no change of clothes, so I left him dissatisfied and came away. Here is a letter to prove it, though I do not know if you will be able to read his writing, for it is worse than my own. Do not show it to anybody or say anything, and please let me have it back." Soon afterwards, indeed, he did paint a portrait of Saavedra.

The technique and pictorial conception of this work are the same as in the portrait of Jovellanos, as are the feeling of space and the general arrangement of the paintings.

Goya's great work in 1798, however, was the decoration of San Antonio de la Florida. The hermitage owes its name to the fact that it was built on an old estate called "La Florida" belonging to the Marqués de Castel Rodrigo. The estate was acquired by Carlos IV in 1792 and the construction of the church, which was placed in an extensive park, was begun immediately and finished in 1798. As regards the decoration executed by Goya, the account for the materials used, dated on 20th December, is still preserved. On 15th June he had received the first delivery of colours and tools. Also preserved is the note of the expense of hiring a coach to convey him between his house, at No. 1, Calle del Desengaño, and the hermitage, at 52 *reales* a day. Judging by this account, the painting of the hermitage was begun on 1st August and completed in one hundred and twenty days. The number of days on which Goya actually painted was certainly less than this. We may recall that he had painted in forty days the great cupola of El Pilar, which was considerably larger in area than the whole of the decoration of San Antonio de la Florida.

The year 1799 saw the publication of the *Caprichos*, a series of eighty etchings preceded by the *Self-portrait*, which was put on sale on 6th February. Fifteen days later, when twenty-seven sets had already been sold, at the price of an ounce of gold each, the edition was withdrawn, possibly through the influence of the Inquisition or from fear of its intervention. Twenty years later Goya, then a refugee in Bordeaux, wrote to Joaquín Ferrer: "The *Caprichos*... I gave to the King...; and yet I was denounced to the Holy (Inquisition)." In this series Goya reached one of the peaks of his art, the one most closely related to the popular spirit and that which really made him internationally famous, by reason of its direct and spontaneous narrative character, but also because of the representation of the dramatic, absurd and strange. Scenes of witchcraft are combined with moral and social satire, visions of the gallows, the world of the *maja*, the procuress, the rake, the rogue and the beggar. In some scenes Goya takes pleasure in representing human beings with the features of animals. Short, penetrating captions accompany the drawings, adding to their mordacity and making the artist's intention quite specific. In later series Goya was frequently to indulge this fancy for adding these brief but pointed literary accompaniments to his drawings.

In the same year Goya painted the portrait of the doctor and French Ambassador to Madrid, *Fernand Guillemardet*, that of the *Marquesa de Santa Cruz*, that of his colleague *José Camarón* and that of the *Marqués de Bondad Real*. From a reference in Moratin's diary we know that in July Goya was painting that writer's portrait, a sober work combining very soft modelling with strict precision of drawing, which now hangs in the Academy of San Fernando. The Duke and Duchess of Osuna continued to collect Goyas, and in 1799 they bought, for the "Alameda", seven small genre paintings representing *The Meadow, The Four Seasons* and two country scenes. We have, in fact, already studied them as the preliminary sketches for tapestry cartoons, which Goya probably kept in his studio.

On 24th September, Queen María Luisa wrote to Godoy telling him that Goya was working on a portrait of her wearing a mantilla. This is the full-length portrait that hangs in the Royal Palace, companion piece to the portrait of *Carlos IV in Shooting Clothes*, in which the King wears a coat covered with bright flecks and is portrayed with a smiling, good-natured countenance. In the same letter she says that when she went to the Escorial Goya was to paint a portrait of her on horseback, "for I want him to paint Marcial". Marcial was the name of her favourite horse, a present from Godoy.

This renewed contact with the King and Queen, in intimate surroundings removed from their Court at Madrid, brought Goya the eagerly desired post of *Primer Pintor de Cámara* (First Painter to the Chamber), on 31st October. At the same time Mariano Salvador Maella, a veteran artist and an old friend of Goya's, was also appointed *Primer Pintor de Cámara*.

At this time Goya was very often working for the royal family at La Granja, the Escorial or Aranjuez, the country seats preferred by the sovereigns for their holidays. The correspondence between the Queen and Godoy provides us with further interesting information. In the letters written from the Escorial in October the Queen writes: "I have spent two and a half hours perched on a platform..., with a hat on"; and a few days later: "The portrait on horseback is finished, as far as I am concerned in it, after three sittings, and they say it is even more like than the one with the mantilla." This must refer to the splendid painting of María Luisa on horseback; the *Fig. 63* accompanying equestrian portrait of the King was probably painted at the same time. In these works *Figs. 64-65* the artist stressed the monumental character, contrasting the great mass of the figures with a stark sky which seems to be retreating into the background.

A letter written by the Queen on 24th April tells us that Goya was then painting the portrait of *The Condesa de Chinchón*, the wife of Godoy. Doña María Teresa de Borbón, daughter of the *Fig. 66* Infante Luis, was that little girl Goya had known and portrayed at Arenas de San Pedro sixteen years before. This portrait is one of the finest examples of Goya's undeniable genius for revealing the feminine world and endowing it with the most captivating pictorial qualities.

After finishing this portrait, Goya began one of his most important works, the great and deservedly famous composition of *The Family of Carlos IV*. *Figs. 68 to 70*

In this work, one of the most important in all Spanish painting, he succeeded not only in portraying his personages and their age, but also in creating a human document of the first importance. Goya refrained from idealizing reality and even gave the picture an exaggeratedly mordant treatment. Perhaps the secret of the greatness of this painting is its profound humanity, both as a whole and in each of the figures that go to make it up. Apart, of course, from the innovations in technique and the exquisitely beautiful colour harmonies, based on reddish browns, pale golds, whites and yellowish tints, offset by vivid touches of red. Following the example of Velázquez, Goya included a portrait of himself in the background of the painting, basing it on the impressive *Self-Portrait* in which he is wearing spectacles, now in the Museum of Castres. *Fig. 67*

To 1801, too, belongs the portrait of *Godoy* represented as a general in the war with Portugal, *Figs. 71-72* the "War of the Oranges", as it was called, which had broken out on 27th February. This portrait shows the royal favourite with the standards added to his coat-of-arms on 7th July. It is a picture in which Goya combines the grand official portrait in the French manner with the drama of a battle scene, which serves as a background. The head of the sitter, moreover, is an extraordinary portrait, harmonising the rather soft features of the face with the somewhat relaxed pose of the figure. The horses in the background are forerunners of those that appear in the *Second of May*. Sánchez Cantón has pointed out that this portrait must have been painted before 4th October 1801, the date on which Godoy received the title of Generalissimo of Land and Sea, with its insignia of a blue sash, for in this painting he still wears the red band of Captain General.

In 1802 the Duchess of Alba died. Goya contributed to the project for the funerary monument with a drawing representing three veiled figures bearing the Duchess's body to its interment in a pyramid-shaped tomb that appears in the background. According to Ezquerra del Bayo, the projected mausoleum was probably erected in the crypt of the oratory of the Padres del Salvador in Madrid and would have been pulled down in 1842 when the Duchess's remains were transferred to their present resting place in the cemetery of La Sacramental de San Pedro y San Andrés.

In 1803 Goya painted the portraits of the *Conde and Condesa de Fernán Núñez*. In the splendour *Figs. 73 and 74* of their colouring and the brilliance of their execution, they are among the finest of his portraits. Goya places his sitters in the countryside, bringing out their youthfulness and the distinctive characteristics of their class. In the portrait of the young lady, he emphasizes the stylized attitude of the figure seated on the ground and offers a splendid example of the freedom and invention of his technique. In a letter addressed by the painter to Miguel Cayetano Soler, dated 9th October 1803, he makes a reference to "the copy of the portrait of Your Excellency made by Esteve..." The present whereabouts of this painting is unfortunately unknown.

In this same year Goya offered to make over to the King the engraved plates of the *Caprichos* and the two hundred and forty sets left unsold. The offer was accepted on 9th October, in exchange for a life pension of twelve thousand *reales* a year in favour of the painter's son, Javier. In the same year Goya bought a house in the Calle de los Reyes in Madrid, of which he took possession on 13th June, for a sum of eighty thousand *reales*, a purchase made not with the intention of his living in the house but as an investment.

In spite of his deafness, Goya applied in 1804 for the post of Director General of the Academy. The voting went against him and Gregorio Ferro was given the post. It is interesting to recall that it was this same mediocre painter who defeated Goya in his first unsuccessful candidature in an Academy competition, in December 1763. On this later occasion it would seem, however, that it was not on grounds of artistic ability, or from any prejudice on the part of the Academicians, that Goya's application was turned down, but on account of his deafness, which, however highly they may have regarded him as an artist, would have made it impossible for him to assume the directorship of an Academy of the Arts. Nevertheless, the failure must have come as a shock to Goya, and it appears to have urged him to even greater activity, which is evidenced by his prodigious output in the years immediately following this event.

Fig. 75 At this time he signed the portrait of the *Marquesa de Santiago* and that of her husband, the *Marqués de San Adrián*, a masterly work, in the same key as the portrait of *The Conde de Fernán Núñez*, but with an increased refinement of execution, with its superb painterly qualities and the fine harmony of its composition based on the treatment of the light and shade of the background. It is appropriate here to draw attention to a characteristic of Goya's works at this time, which is that they display a dual fluctuation: on the one hand there is an evident awareness of entering another age, an awareness that becomes more noticeable at the turn of the century; and, on the other hand, Goya's innate nonconformity is more in evidence. His paintings display a greater or lesser inspiration according to his feeling for the subject, resulting in a certain inequality in his work which, though it does not affect the consistent technical quality, comes out in the summary or rough treatment of certain details.

The year 1805 was that of the Battle of Trafalgar, a momentous year for Spain and for Goya one of the most brilliant periods of his career. The Academy of History commissioned him to paint the portrait of their Director, the Naval Officer *José de Vargas Ponce*. In a letter of 8th January, Vargas Ponce asks Ceán Bermúdez if he will approach the artist to persuade him to paint the portrait "as he does when he wants to". It is a very good portrait, although one of his simpler compositions, representing the sitter in bust-length and without showing the hands. Goya received a higher fee for portraits including hands, and according to tradition he was often to declare that to paint hands demanded as much work as to paint the face. Everything in Vargas Ponce's portrait evokes a sense of quiet energy, and in this respect the modelling of the uniform — or the small part that appears in the painting — is extraordinarily effective.

Figs. 76-77 In 1805 Goya signed and dated one of the two versions, both by his hand, of the portrait of the *Marquesa de Santa Cruz*, Doña Joaquina Téllez Girón, daughter of the Duke and Duchess of Osuna. Goya had already painted her when she was a little girl in the family portrait now in the Prado. On 7th July of this same year the marriage of Javier Goya to Gumersinda Goicoechea took place. The occasion is commemorated in the wonderful pair of full-length portraits of the betrothed. Javier's portrait reflects a father's affection for his son, whom Goya saw as a model of distinction and almost foppish elegance. At any rate we are presented with a figure of extreme refinement, with all the characteristics of contemporary dandyism. The bride is more naturalistic in treatment and less arresting, but the result is still an excellent portrait. A short while after the wedding Goya apparently painted the series of miniature portraits of the members of Javier's new family.

In the year 1806 the political situation in Spain was complicated by Godoy's ambitious schemes for subjugating part of Portugal with the idea of making a small kingdom for himself, a scheme in which he counted on the tacit approval of Carlos IV. Since this project did not fit in with Napoleon's plans, Godoy made overtures to the anti-Bonaparte coalition, but France intervened and obliged Spain to collaborate with her by sending fifteen thousand troops to Germany and Denmark, under the command of the Marqués de La Romana. The internal situation of the country was also becoming more chaotic every day. A faction opposed to Godoy was formed under the protection of the Prince of Asturias, the heir apparent to the Spanish throne and future King Fernando VII, and under the command of the Dukes of San Carlos and El Infantado. In reading the history of this fateful period for Spain, we constantly come across names and personalities known to us from Goya's portraits. We find Goya painting the portraits of the leading personalities of the time, irrespective of the political faction or group to which they might belong. And the time was soon to come when he would also depict in his paintings, drawings and engravings the tragic culmination of historical events, leaving to posterity the most devastating records of the age.

We begin our brief examination of the portraits dated in 1806 with that of *Tadeo Bravo*, which bears an elaborate dedication. This is another instance of a work carried out as an obligation incidental to Goya's aristocratic commissions. To be counted among the latter are the brilliant portraits of *Fig. 78* *Antonio Porcel* and his wife, *Isabel Cobos*, both superbly executed and possessing formal splendour and perfect characterization. The portrait of Isabel Cobos is one of the most universally admired of Goya's paintings, as much for the richness of the forms and the beautiful harmony of colour as for the physical attraction of the sitter, who has become through this painting an essential figure in the repertory of universally admired Spanish female types. It is clear that with Goya the personality of the sitter to some extent affected the general impression and meaning of the painting, as we may see in the simple and beautiful portrait of *Sabasa García*, with the airy ringlets covering her forehead and the quiet intensity of her gaze.

Fig. 79

We have now come to the appropriate point for considering the famous pair of paintings, the *Naked Maja* and *Clothed Maja*, which have been mistakenly associated with the Duchess of Alba and the novelettish elaborations of her relationship with Goya indulged in by certain authors. It would seem, in fact, that the two *Majas* were painted for Godoy, since they are included in the inventory made on the occasion of the attachment of his estate in January 1808. It is our conclusion that they were painted only shortly before that date and that they belong to the period 1803-1806 under discussion. The general conception of the two paintings, as well as their technique and palette, corresponds very closely to what we have observed in our examination of the works of this period.

Figs. 81 and 82-83

The representation of the nude figure suggested to Goya the use of a firm yet supple handling and a modelling of almost imperceptible modulation of tone that contains the form within a fairly well-defined contour. The evocation of the flesh is complete; both a truthful representation and an idealized portrayal of feminine beauty are achieved, and the result is one of the greatest representations of the nude in the history of art. There is, as it were, a preoccupation with softness throughout the painting. The faithful rendering of the material details of the couch — especially of the cushions with their lace edgings, which are rendered with a subtle play of shadows and evoke a real sense of the weight and pressure of the body upon them — is one of the most significant characteristics of the painting; and equally, perhaps, the soft lighting that caresses the woman's body, set against a background which, to avoid any strong contrasts, is not very dark. The clothed *Maja*, on the other hand, is painted with great bravura, with more vivid lights and stronger contrasts, and with those rapid, dashed-in strokes of heavy paint that suggest the actual substance and relief of the material — especially apparent in the handling of the bolero. This figure, with its combination of naturalism and idealization, still displays something of that archaic, puppet-like quality observed in connection with the more effective of the female figures in the later tapestry cartoons. The dress of the clothed *Maja* gives the painting an air of the period, and accordingly makes it less timeless than its unclothed counterpart.

The mythological painting of *Psyche and Cupid* would also seem to fit most comfortably into this period. It was apparently a commissioned work, painted with little enthusiasm, and could be regarded as an essay in what is called the "Empire Style". Psyche's facial resemblance to the two *Majas* is so close as to suggest that the same model was used.

Fig. 80

An extremely interesting group of works possibly belonging to this period is that of the five panels in the Academy of San Fernando in Madrid: *Flagellants, Madhouse, Bullfight, Tribunal of the Inquisition* and *Burial of the Sardine*. These truly outstanding paintings have in common a turbulence of form and an instinctive variety of new plastic concepts, and Goya was inspired to introduce pictorial solutions in all of them and to give a unity to each painting through the organization and rhythm of the composition. The result is a series of masterpieces of astounding modernity. Some of the paintings depict veritable "pandemonia", and in these the Goya of the *Caprichos* and witchcraft scenes seems to find himself in his element again. One may also observe in the *Bullfight* distortions of the forms to express the movement — or rather the acceleration of movement — of the character running after the bull, and the remarkable way in which Goya suggests the crowd of spectators by means of mere touches, flicks and dashes of colour and light. On the other hand, the bull in this painting is treated realistically, as if Goya delighted in recording its individual line and aspect. The *Flagellants* and the *Tribunal of the Inquisition* deal with some of Goya's most celebrated themes, concerning that face of Spain often referred to — with exaggeration rather than untruth — as "Black Spain". In these works there persists something of the freedom of expression indulged in by the medieval artist when depicting devout types. The satire is evident, as also the artist's infinite skill in creating the far from noble facial types and expressions, in which he employs the minimum of drawing and painting. Parts of the paintings, especially of the *Flagellants*, are left "unfinished": as he seeks to give the greatest impact to a form, he leaves it at the moment when he has achieved this impact, realizing instinctively that the "unfinished" form can be more dramatic than the detailed description.

Figs. 84 to 90

The Peninsular War, the House of the Deaf Man and Bordeaux (1807-1828)

Godoy's perfidious obstinacy on the one hand and Napoleon's ruthless policies on the other continued in 1807 to make plans for the partition of Portugal, which was finally decided by the Treaty of Fontainebleau on 27th October 1807. The French troops entered Spain by the Basque frontier, but the conspiring friends of Prince Fernando attempted to rouse popular feeling against them. The King discovered the plot, denounced it to the nation and arrested his son, who did not long delay in betraying his followers. This led to the so-called "Proceso del Escorial", the Escorial Trial, which ended in the pardoning of the participants in the plot. Meanwhile, the vanguard of General Junot's French army reached Lisbon on 30th November.

It is not surprising that in this anxious time of war Goya should have seen his commissions waning. There are some portraits dated in 1807: the vigorous and spontaneously painted portrait of his friend the actor *Isidoro Máiquez*, and the portraits of the politician *Antonio Marqués Caballero* and his wife, neither very distinguished personalities. It is clear that this meagre number of paintings does not represent his entire output for the year. Alone in his studio and isolated by his deafness, Goya would no doubt have spent these troubled days painting and drawing from his imagination.

1808 was a year of war and disaster for Spain. Under the pretext of invading Portugal, and with the blessing of the Spanish Crown and Government, the French troops continued to pour into the Peninsula. Dupont's men were in Valladolid in January, Moncey's in Burgos; and other columns from Perpignan occupied the fortresses of Figueras and Barcelona. Complete confusion reigned in the country, and the feeling of hostility to Godoy spread. A well-intentioned but belated move on Godoy's part provoked the Insurrection of Aranjuez on 17th March.

This popular uprising, instigated by the supporters of the Prince of Asturias, demanded the abdication of Carlos IV and the trial of Godoy.

Fernando VII entered Madrid in triumph on 24th March. The city was occupied by Murat's troops, who had made their triumphal entry on the preceding day. On the 28th of the month, the Academy of San Fernando requested Goya to paint the portrait of the new King, in spite of the fact that the painter had not attended the meetings of the Academy for some time. To satisfy Goya's request to make preliminary studies from life, Fernando VII sat for him for a few minutes on 6th and 7th April.

The tragic political events continued. Napoleon, in preparation for his seizure of the Crown, succeeded in luring the new King, the ex-king Carlos IV, his wife María Luisa and Godoy to Bayonne, where they remained virtually prisoners of the Emperor. Fernando VII was offered the Crown of Etruria, but was persuaded by the Spanish grandees in his retinue to refuse. Meanwhile, in Madrid, the young Princes resisted Murat's order that they leave for Bayonne, whereupon on 2nd May the populace demonstrated in their favour, and there followed the desperate attack against the Mamelukes in the Puerta del Sol and the terrible reprisals which ended with the executions of 3rd May, events which Goya was later to immortalize in his two famous pictures in the Prado. The news of these events reached Bayonne and caused even greater confusion among the members of the Royal Family, a confusion which was exploited by Napoleon to procure the abdication of Fernando VII and the final resignation of the old King. It was Godoy who was the author of the pact of abdication of the whole Bourbon family. Meanwhile, in Madrid, Murat formed an Assembly to govern Spain under his presidency.

In June an assembly of representatives of Spain and her colonies met in Bayonne to approve the new constitution planned on the Napoleonic pattern and with Joseph Bonaparte as king and head of a new hereditary monarchy. A government was formed to include past statesmen, some of whom appear in Goya's repertoire of portraits.

Joseph Bonaparte entered Madrid on 20th July and a little later wrote to Napoleon: "My position is unique: I have not a single supporter"; an accurate observation, which he was to reaffirm in another letter dated four days later: "You are mistaken; your glory will be demolished in Spain." In the event, realizing that his position in Madrid had become precarious after the Battle of Bailén (22nd July), he retired across the River Ebro. Everywhere local assemblies sprang up to prepare for an uprising. Envoys were sent secretly to London and attacks were made on the French troops, who found themselves obliged to raise the siege of Zaragoza. The English under the command of Wellington disembarked in Portugal, and the Marqués de La Romana's Spanish troops succeeded in being repatriated through Sweden. On 25th September the "Supreme Junta for the Government of the Realm" was set up in Aranjuez, under the presidency of Floridablanca.

The Academy held its usual annual exhibition this year, at which Goya showed his portrait of *Máiquez*, painted in the previous year, and the portrait of the sculptor *José Folch de Cardona*, now lost. The portrait of *Pantaleón Pérez de Nenín*, dated in 1808, displays a great ease and a marked naturalism. In a letter of 2nd October Goya says that the portrait of *Fernando VII* is finished and declares that "the Royal Academy will pardon the defects in the said portrait, taking into consideration that His Majesty only gave me three-quarters of an hour on two occasions". An amount of 150 doubloons was agreed as payment for the painting, but never materialized.

At this time Goya asked for leave of absence to visit Zaragoza. It seems that Palafox, the General in command of the garrison, called him there to commemorate in a painting, inspired by the ruins of the city, its victorious defence against the Napoleonic troops. Goya arrived in Zaragoza at the end of October 1808 and made a number of sketches, one of which depicted some boys dragging along the main street the French soldiers killed in the attack of 4th August. These sketches are unfortunately lost, having been painted over lest they should fall into the hands of the French — who were soon to take possession of the city — and it has not yet been possible to remove the overpainting. In November the painter left for Fuendetodos and later returned to Madrid.

Towards the end of the year Napoleon's counter-attack began, and after the capitulation of Madrid, on 4th December, Joseph I was reinstalled on the throne. Goya was among the thirty thousand heads of families who signed their names to the document of 23rd December, swearing love and allegiance to the French King. The Central Junta fled to Seville and the struggle was continued by civilian guerrilla fighters, by men of the people, by priests, who looked upon it as a holy war, and by members of the lesser nobility. One of the most famous of the guerrillas was *"El Empecinado"*, whom Goya was to portray some years later.

Fig. 113

In the spring of 1809 the English, under the command of Arthur Wellesley, later Duke of Wellington, again disembarked in Portugal and began a tenacious struggle that was finally to be rewarded with victory. Haphazard and persistent attacks and skirmishes of the guerrilla forces were taking place in every corner of Spain.

In 1810 Madrid was in a state of apparent calm, in the midst of what was for the Spaniards their struggle against the armies of Napoleon. Life continued under the vigilance of the French occupation, and all citizens, some more, some less, had gradually come to collaborate in some way or another. Sympathy for certain liberal reforms gave rise to the so-called *"afrancesados"*, or French sympathizers, who were prepared to assist in bringing into effect the new ideas and forms of government, different from those of absolute monarchy, if not to assist in keeping Joseph I on the throne. Goya, who was later to be accused as a collaborator, may serve as an example of the *"afrancesado"* who, without forgetting the brutalities committed by the French in repressing the patriotic Spanish resistance, was inclined for the good of the country to place himself at the disposal of the "intruder" King in so far as it might seem to foster the spirit of liberalism and reform of Napoleon's creed.

On 27th February Goya had finished the large allegorical composition commissioned by the Town Council of Madrid in honour of Joseph I, which was subsequently to be changed to commemorate the heroes of 2nd May. He also took part, probably unwillingly, in the selection of fifty paintings by Old Masters to be sent to Paris as a contribution towards the formation of the Napoleon Museum. On 15th June he attended the reception into the Academy of San Fernando of the Marqués de Almenara, appointed Protector of the Academy by the King.

At the same time Goya continued to paint portraits, including some intimate portraits of his friends, like the pair representing his son's parents-in-law, *Martín de Goicoechea* and *Juana Galarza*, executed in a very fluid technique. In a very different technique are the two portraits of the French General *Nicolas Guye* and his nephew, *Victor Guye*, executed in heavy paint and with a spirited brush.

Fig. 91

The only information concerning his domestic life is the will made jointly with his wife on 3rd June. Although references to his public life are comparatively numerous in this year (1810), it is reasonable to suppose that as his loneliness grew his activity increased too, spurred by his inexhaustible creative impulse. We know that in these days of the French occupation he engraved some of the plates of the *Disasters of War*, his second great series of etchings, which was to be finally completed some years later.

Figs. 97 to 100

To return to the course of political events, the patriotic resistance continued all over Spain, and in the parts not under French domination this resistance began to be properly organized. On 24th September the *Cortes*, or Parliament, established on the Isle of León off the coast of Cadiz, issued a general decree for the reorganization of the Spanish resistance. It proposed the union of all the forces opposed to the intruder king and the reinstatement on the throne of Fernando VII. But in this time of bitter conflict, when no quarter was given, liberal ideas had the commanding voice. The *Cortes* of Cadiz insisted above all that sovereignty belonged, not to the Council of the Regency, nor to the King, but to Parliament. This attitude, as may be seen, both opposed the invader and utilized any advantage that might be derived from his ideas of reform.

In 1811 the French troops continued to lay siege to the towns and the guerrilla warfare continued unabated. The rule of Joseph I carried on with a certain stability, and life in Madrid maintained a degree of outward calm. Goya has not left us a single work dated in this year, but it would seem to have been, nevertheless, one of the most intensely active years of his career.

In the following year the *Cortes* of Cadiz drew up and published the "Constitution of 1812". In a liberal and constructive spirit, surprising in those times of complete upheaval and considering the long-established tradition of absolutism, the whole system of government of the country was reshaped. Meanwhile, the body of the English army under the command of the future Duke of Wellington, which for many months had been actively engaged in Portugal, began its offensive against the Napoleonic forces, starting with the relief of Ciudad Rodrigo and Badajoz and later the victory of Los Arapiles, and finally liberating Madrid on 12th August.

At this time Goya was anxiously following the rapid development of events and, isolated in his deafness, was working incessantly, experimenting with new methods to widen the scope of his powerful imaginative gifts. He continued to follow the path taken during the months of his convalescence in 1793, which he so succinctly expressed in his letter to Moratín at the time, and which was to take him, as we shall see, to the total discovery of his own world of imagination, both in the subject-matter of his paintings and in its treatment. Another misfortune, the loss of his faithful and silent wife, Josefa Bayeu, who died on 20th June, increased his isolation, his voluntary and active seclusion in his house on the Calle del Desengaño — the "Street of Disillusion" — a designation very appropriate to Goya's mental humour in his later years. Javier, living his insignificant life away from his father, with his small private income and no known occupation, now came to claim his mother's inheritance. He came, in effect, to take away half of what, over so many years of tireless and unrelenting work, his father had managed to save out of his modest official salary and the fees paid by his niggardly clientele and the occasional, not overgenerous, protector. We may recall that only two years before the painter and his wife had drawn up a will, and according to the law of Castile the son, as his mother's heir, was entitled to half the property acquired by the family during the marriage; and since Goya married Bayeu's sister at the very beginning of his career, this was in effect the only property he possessed. By mutual agreement, an inventory was drawn up and the separate items were assessed by professional valuers. This document was published on 28th October.

The share of the effects adjudicated to Goya comprised the furniture and linen, a gold clock and part of the silver and jewellery, together with a considerable sum of money. The son became the owner of the house on the Calle de Valverde, the library and the collection of paintings and engravings. This seemingly illogical sharing of the effects may well be a sign of Goya's quiet slyness. By adjudicating to his son a collection of paintings, which had no value in ready money at the time, he could perhaps ensure that they stayed in his house, as indeed turned out to be the case. While the paintings remained in his father's house, however, Javier did not on that account neglect to make sure that they would come to him, and accordingly he marked each one with the sign of a large "X", standing for Xavier (Javier), followed by the inventory number. This declaration of ownership, while it is hardly consistent with a feeling of real affection and trust between father and son, has provided us with invaluable historical evidence, thanks to which it has been possible to identify a large number of the paintings that were in Goya's possession in 1812.

We shall now consider some of the paintings that were listed in the deed of partition of Goya's effects between the artist and his son:

The Inventory number 23 is still clearly visible on the painting depicting a vain old woman accompanied by her hideous maid and preening herself beneath Time's menacing broom. It is one of the well-known pair of paintings in the Lille Museum. This picture, so unpleasant in its subject *Fig. 95* yet so beautiful as a painting, appears in the Inventory under the title *Time*. A resemblance has been noticed between Queen María Luisa in later life and the old woman seated before her hand-mirror on the back of which is written the legend: *Qué tal?* ("How are things?"), comparable to the captions that accompany the plates of the *Caprichos*. Furthermore, the hair-ornament in the form of an arrow is similar to that described in the Queen's correspondence with Godoy and to the ornament she wears in the large group portrait of the *Family of Carlos IV*. While there is a facial resemblance, the exaggerated rendering of old age in the toothless countenance of the old woman in the Lille painting, with its sunken and emaciated flesh taken almost to the point of decomposition, gives a more generalized character to the image. It may well have been painted after the enforced abdication of Carlos IV and the Queen in 1807. The second of the two Lille paintings, *Fig. 94* *The Letter*, probably a pair to the preceding one, is even more daring in its approach.

Fig. 93 Very similar in concept and treatment is the *Majas on a Balcony*, a work which was identified by Enriqueta Frankfort thanks to an old photographical reproduction in which the Inventory number 24 appears clearly visible in the lower left-hand corner. The contrast between the near plane, in which the two young women sit, luminous and detailed in treatment, and the second plane, which contains their sombre male companions wrapped in cloaks, could hardly be more pronounced. However, these two planes in depth, each with its distinct tonal and surface treatment, are given an inextricable unity by their formal treatment and rhythm. Each *maja* is connected with her companion by the correspondence of outline of the figures; and this unification by pairs is reinforced by the correspondence in attitude and by the echoing rhythm of each pair of heads. Of this painting, now in the Metropolitan Museum of New York, there is a replica, whose present whereabouts is unknown, but which would seem to be from Goya's hand and may possibly be even more poignant in its expression.

The Inventory number 25 appears on the remarkable painting recently published under the title *El Garrotillo* (The Croup) and interpreted as a representation of a physician roughly treating a boy *Fig. 92* suffering from this ailment. In the Inventory, however, the painting is described as *Lazarillo de Tormes*, which reveals its real theme, an illustration of an episode from that famous Spanish picaresque novel. The fact that Goya should have done a painting purely illustrative in character from the popular Spanish classic is evidence of his familiarity with works of literature, which is further confirmed by his predilection for the theme of Celestina and is not without an important bearing on the appreciation of his work.

Fig. 96 We now come to the painting entitled *A giant*, tremendous in its theme (of mythological reference) and splendid in its painting and in the sombre grandeur of the huge figure. The painting is listed under item 18 in the Inventory. It represents a multitude of encamped people, with wagons and cattle, fleeing in panic before the enormous presence of the naked giant that looms above the horizon shrouded in clouds. One may observe the use, here and there, of the palette-knife, and the particular quality of the sharp relief that it permits.

In this painting Goya employs free and irregular brushstrokes and passages left "unfinished", or merely suggesting the forms by means of shading or intensity of colour, whereby he is able to establish the planes of the composition and create an atmosphere of heightened fantasy. We may observe the ingenious introduction of the bank of clouds as a means of transition between the imaginary protagonist of the picture and the reality of the scene in the lower foreground, full of incident.

Goya did not execute the foregoing paintings as commissioned works, but to satisfy his own powerful, creative and expressive urge to paint, which called forth more profound qualities.

But in this brief biography of Goya we should also mention other works dated in this year, 1812. In the middle of August, a few days after the liberation of Madrid by the combined British and Spanish forces, Goya was commissioned to paint the portrait of the future *Duke of Wellington*, at that time Commander-in-Chief of the allied armies. A drawing in red chalk and a preliminary oil study from life for the painting exist, from which Goya painted a half-length portrait and the large canvas depicting the Duke on horseback, the latter exhibited to the public at the Academy in this year.

But the rejoicing of the Spaniards was to be short-lived; on 3rd November the French recaptured Madrid and Joseph I returned to the capital. A work probably executed during this year of terrible conflict is the large painting of the *Assumption of the Virgin*, on the High Altar of the parish church of Chinchon, which states on the back that it was put in place in the 13th June 1812. We may recall that one of the priests of the church was Goya's brother Camilo.

We do not know a single work by Goya dated in 1813.

Under the pressure of the allied troops commanded by Wellington, the situation of the French in Madrid became precarious. The King, Joseph Bonaparte, felt it wise to retire and transferred his Court to Valladolid. A clear sign of defeatism was the order he gave to the famous convoy, with its cargo of works of art and other precious objects looted from Spanish churches and palaces, to make for the frontier. As it happened, however, the convoy was to be intercepted and captured by Wellington, who at the Battle of Vitoria gained the final victory and the expulsion of the intruder king. Napoleon found himself forced to make a pact with his prisoner, Fernando VII, and on 11th December 1813 signed the Treaty of Valençay, by which he again recognised Fernando as King of Spain, on condition that he ordered the English out of the country and respected the "afrancesados" (those who had collaborated with the French under the occupation), and also that he concluded a commercial treaty with France.

The country, impoverished by six years of war, disorganized, bristling with political rivalries, and with the army and the people divided between the supporters of liberalism and the conservative factions, was offered as its only hope of salvation a treacherous king, egotistical, corrupt and bigoted, who had spent his years of captivity in France fawning on Napoleon and sending him congratulations on his triumphs and victories in Spain. By an irony of fate he was to be hailed as *El Deseado* (The Desired One).

On 6th January 1814 a Council of the Regency was set up in Madrid, composed of Cardinal Luis de Borbón and two generals. On the 24th, Goya addressed a memorandum to the Regents requesting financial help in order that he might "commemorate by his brush the most notable and heroic deeds... against the tyrant of Europe". Thus commences the history of two of Goya's most famous paintings: *The Attack on the Mamelukes* (also known as *The Second of May*) and *The Third of May*, representing the executions by firing squad at La Moncloa. Two preparatory oil-studies exist for the first composition, rapidly sketched in with impulsive brushstrokes and an agitated rhythm, which betray the painter's endeavours to unite and articulate the forms. The final painting, in addition to achieving this intimate fusion of the forms, heightens the sense of grandeur and emotion of the scene. The painter looks beyond any mere recounting of the event and captures it with all the reality and immediacy of the tragedy. The shooting scene, on the other hand, is a solid composition, as clear and direct as a poster, but is given concentration and intensity by the simplicity of the forms and colours. Ochres, white, black and grey predominate in this painting, and are as grandly expressive as the strong, simple and direct organization of the two groups in the foreground, the riflemen and their victims respectively. Goya also painted at this time the portrait of *Palafox*. *Figs. 102 to 105* *Fig. 101*

Fernando VII, accompanied by his small court of followers in captivity, entered Spain by the Catalan frontier on 22nd March. A few weeks later there began the silent contest between the absolutist ambitions of the King, supported by a group of reactionary military men and aristocrats, and the spirit of liberalism that had informed the drawing up of the "Constitution of Cadiz". Prosecutions and imprisonments followed, and an investigation of liberals and "*afrancesados*" was instituted. Thus commenced the first of the large-scale emigrations which were to characterize Spain's political history in the nineteenth century. Fernando VII arrived in Madrid on 7th May; the persecutions increased, and more fled the country. Among those who left Spain for good were such outstanding figures as Meléndez Valdés and Moratín. The Court of the Inquisition was brought back. Punishments were arbitrary and terrifying. Spain had lost her influence and prestige and at the Congress of Vienna her great sacrifices during the Napoleonic Wars availed her nothing. At home, the excesses of the absolute monarchy provoked liberal counter-proclamations. Finally, the event of surpassing historical moment took place: the revolt of Spain's American colonies, which a few years later were to obtain their independence.

Through these days of political confusion and social disruption Goya continued painting in Madrid. The only work actually dated in 1814 is the portrait of his friend and assistant, the Valencian painter *Ascensió Juliá*.

The scarcity of references to Goya in the year 1815 is compensated for by the large number of works he produced, extremely original and abounding in splendid effects. This year witnessed Goya's return to normality as a painter of Madrid society. In July he was paid by the governing body of the Imperial Canal of Aragon, in Zaragoza, for a portrait of *Fernando VII* and one of the *Duke of San Carlos*, a friend of the young King who had accompanied him into exile. *Figs. 108-109* *Fig. 111*

Fig. 110

Fig. 107
Fig. 106

Fig. 112

Fig. 114
Fig. 115

Fig. 116

Fig. 117

Also dated in 1815 is the *Self-Portrait* in the Academy of San Fernando, of which variants exist in the Prado and the Museum of Northampton, Massachusetts. Other works of this year exhibit great originality, as, for instance, the portrait of the musician *Fray Juan Fernández de Rojas*, penetrating, alive and full of humanity. The portrait of *Ignacio de Omulryan* is a real display of painterly effects, produced by contrasting the simplicity and severity of the face with the finely resolved tonal harmony of the whole. The list of portraits painted in this year is completed by those of *Fray Miguel Fernández*, who had just been consecrated Bishop of Marcopilis, the South American politician *Lardizábal, José Luis Munárriz* (a work of remarkable power), the engraver *Rafael Esteve*, with its nervous and rapid brushstrokes, which model the forms in the manner of a chalk drawing, and the composer *Quijano*, in which the freedom of execution and general conception anticipate Romantic painting.

To 1816 belong two portraits of exceptional quality: that of the *Tenth Duke of Osuna* and that of his sister, the *Duchess of Abrantes*. It may be mentioned that these were the last portraits of the nobility to be painted by Goya. The reasons for this are not exactly known, but may be conjectured. Possibly Goya's growing repugnance for the renewed advance of absolutism had something to do with it; or his inability to simulate any longer sentiments that he could not feel. Or it could be that the aristocracy and middle classes had come to react against the advanced character of the elderly artist's new painting. It was at this time, too, that another star appeared on the artistic horizon of Madrid, in the person of the painter Vicente López. There now begins for Goya a period of withdrawal. He makes a break with a number of his connections. No longer does he attend the meetings of the Academy. Alone in his house in the Calle del Desengaño, he was probably busily engaged on the final plates for the engraved series of the *Disasters of War* and the *Tauromaquia*. He was also to investigate new pictorial techniques, in which the cane palette-knife appears to have been used in most parts. In 1818 Goya painted what was to be his last work for the Royal Palace in Madrid, the *Saint Elizabeth Comforting a Sick Child*.

On 27th February 1819 Goya bought, for the sum of sixty thousand *reales*, a property on the outskirts of Madrid, near the Toledo Bridge. This country house, surrounded by some twenty acres of land, was to be immortalized under the name of *La Quinta del Sordo* (The House of the Deaf Man). It is known that in this same year he started work on the conversion of the property as his own dwelling.

In May 1819 Goya was commissioned to paint the large composition of *The Last Communion of Saint Joseph of Calasanz* for one of the altars of the Piarist church of San Antón in Madrid, where it was put in place in the following August. This impressive painting follows the preparatory oil study almost literally, indicating that Goya had already conceived in his first study the precise effect he desired. The pathos of the expressions is perfectly expressed, while the colours are almost entirely restricted to whites and reds, which heighten the effect of the dominant black.

Towards the end of 1819 Goya suffered a serious illness. It appears that he occupied his convalescence making drawings and lithographs and executing the final plates of his last series of etchings, the *Disparates*, which was to remain unfinished. The plates were first published by the Academy in 1864.

We cannot pass over an event incidental to Goya's biography, the death in this year of Carlos IV and María Luisa. These unfortunate and mediocre sovereigns, who have in their favour their appreciation and protection of Goya, died in exile, the King in Naples and the Queen in Rome. The equestrian portraits of the royal couple were the only works by Goya to appear in the first catalogue of the Prado, which opened its doors in November of this year.

1820 was a year of important events in Spain. On 1st January, after a series of frustrated plots and revolts against Fernando's despotic rule, an uprising led by General Riego finally triumphed and the King was forced to accept the Constitution drawn up by the *Cortes* of Cadiz. The ceremony of swearing allegiance to the Constitution took place on 7th March. Prisoners of the Inquisition were freed and this terrible instrument of suppression again disappeared from the Spanish scene.

Meanwhile Goya was convalescing after the illness he had contracted in the previous year. It was at this time that he painted the picture dedicated to his physician, *Goya Being Attended by Dr. Arrieta*, the work in which he attains for the first time the manner characteristic of his last works. This painting, in which he depicts himself in pain, weak and unsteady, comforted and supported by his doctor, was clearly painted during his convalescence.

On 8th April 1820 he attended the Academy to take part in the ceremony of swearing allegiance to the new Constitution, which must have given him great satisfaction, since it represented to Spaniards of his political sympathies the hope of an era of freedom and peace. This new hope may have prompted his decision to decorate his country house, with the thought of spending there the last years of his life, working in tranquillity and for his own satisfaction, for his spirit remained alive and eager. He probably moved into the house immediately after his recovery from his illness and when the work of conversion had been completed. It is fairly certain that his new home was run by Leocadia Zorrilla, a distant relative of the painter, who was to play an important role in the last years of his life. Doña Leocadia, who was separated from her husband, Isidoro Weiss, of German extraction, had a son and daughter; and since the latter, Rosario, was born in 1814, three years after the separation, tradition and Goya's biographers alike have suggested the possibility that the daughter was Goya's. She certainly helped to bring him happiness in his last years of voluntary exile in Bordeaux, where she also became his favourite pupil.

In 1821 Goya was enjoying a period of tranquillity in his country house, cared for by Doña Leocadia and entertained by the games of the little Rosario. He was now ready to do what every great painter dreams of throughout his career: to work for himself alone, giving shape to his passions and dreams through the medium of his colours and forms. He executed the astounding paintings that adorned the walls of the *Quinta del Sordo*, which have passed into history as the *Black Paintings*.   *Figs. 119 to 126* His instinct for the fantastic, confirmed and accentuated from the time of his deafness and translated into images of poignant satirical comment in his witchcraft scenes and the series of drawings and engravings, now reached its highest point. The paintings of the *Quinta* are a synthesis of the monumental forms evolved in his earlier large decorative paintings on the one hand, and his works of fantasy and imagination on the other. The nobly-cast faces derived from classical art undergo terrifying distortions in these paintings. His predilection for a palette restricted to earth colours, black and white is finally stated. The narrative element, though given its proper place, gives way in part to the consideration of form *per se* — and to a recognition of the significance of each and every detail, simplified and intensified to a point at which the paintings may properly qualify as "expressionist". With these paintings Goya decorated the two main rooms of his country house, one on the ground floor and the other on the first floor. His taste for the horrific, his sense of pathos, his emotional temperament and misanthropy and, above all, his pessimism, his need to express those forces which he saw as the terrible and elemental forces of existence: all these things are given their appropriate form in these paintings — in witches and witches' sabbaths, in repulsive senility and savage eroticism, in brutal, elemental combats and village drunkards, and in a Saturn who devours his children, dripping with blood. Technically they are works of supreme achievement, in which Goya's instinctive understanding of the possibilities of a technique that employs the minimum of material resources is exercised to the full; and the final result is no less splendid and impelling for the horrific content of the paintings. They are, in fact, among the most popularized and famous of Goya's works, and have been the subject of many works of scholarship and literary comment.

The arrogant and obstinate Fernando VII had no real intention of submitting to the triumphant tide of liberalism, and did what he could to disrupt the policies of Riego and his associates, thereby fomenting the fratricidal struggle in Spain. In a truly evil moment for the country he enlisted the aid of the Bourbon King of France, Louis XVIII, who dispatched to Spain an army — the so-called "Hundred thousand sons of Saint Louis" — under the command of the Duke of Angoulême. This army entered Spain on 4th April 1823 and, meeting little resistance, took Madrid and restored the absolute monarchy. General Riego was put to death and the executioner's lash and the gallows set to work diligently and quickly. A number of liberals succeeded in fleeing the country.

The persecution of the liberals and their sympathizers continued relentlessly, seeking to eliminate with terrifying ruthlessness both the men and their ideas. Fearing a confiscation of his property, Goya handed over his country house to his only grandson, Mariano Goya, who was at the time seventeen years of age. The deed of transfer was signed on 17th September.

In January 1824, military purge committees were officially set up to examine and put on trial the enemies of the absolutist government. Goya, feeling himself to be in danger, took refuge in the house of the Aragonese Don José Duaso, who was editor of the official *Gazette* and censor. It was there that he painted several works, among them *Group of Old Folk* and a superb portrait   *Fig. 127* of his chance protector, which is dedicated and signed *Por Goya de 78 años* ("By Goya at the age   *Fig. 118* of 78 years"); it was very precisely dated, for his birthday was on 31st March 1824.

These months of hiding must have weakened the artist's spirits; they would spell out to him the magnitude of his fall from a position of favour and fortune, from the time when he painted the family portrait of Carlos IV. Furthermore, he must have missed his old friends, almost all of whom were in exile in France; and he was estranged in spirit from his son, that selfish and listless character who had insisted on legally drawn-up deeds of ownership of his father's paintings. Even his country house, the home he had made for his old age and which he had decorated with so much passion and with so great an expenditure of creative energy, was no longer able to hold him to Spain, now that he had relinquished it to his grandson for fear of reprisals. Everything was beginning to lose meaning for the almost octogenarian genius, and he decided to leave Madrid and the arbitrary and repressive policies of the King. On 2nd May 1824 he applied for six months' leave from his obligations as *Pintor de Cámara* — which in any case he had effectively abandoned — in order to take the waters at Plombières. His application for leave was granted on the 30th of the month, and a few days later he left for France, but instead of making for Plombières went to Bordeaux. One of the last works he executed in Spain is probably the small sketch in black chalk believed to represent Javier Goya and bearing the inscription *Por Goya año 1824* ("By Goya, 1824"). He probably also painted in Madrid, before he left for France, the portrait dated in 1824 and supposed to represent *María Martínez de Puga*, of whom however there is no trace in any references to Goya.

Bordeaux in 1824 was a meeting-place for refugees, among whom was Moratín, the guest, and probably assistant, of another refugee, Manuel Silvela, who had established a school for the Spanish "colony" in the city. Moratín's correspondence with Father Melón offers us a general account of Goya's life in Bordeaux from 27th June of this year onwards. In a letter of that date he describes Goya's arrival in the French city: "Goya has indeed arrived, deaf, old, weary and weak...; very pleased and anxious to see everyone. He has been here three days... I have urged him to return by September and not get stuck in Paris..." Goya did not, in fact, stay in Bordeaux, but continued his journey to the French capital, where, according to a letter from Moratín dated 8th July, he lodged with some distant relatives of the Goicoechea family and stayed until September.

We know very little of Goya's movements in Paris. Yriarte, who makes an error in date, says of the visit: *"Il put assister à l'aurore de la seconde Renaissance française, il vit les œuvres de Gros, Géricault et même celles de Delacroix, qui devait devenir un de ses plus fervents admirateurs: le vieillard redevint jeune pour une heure, se mêla un instant au mouvement romantique, voulut connaître les grands artistes de ce temps-là, et entra même en correspondance avec Horace Vernet"*. This is all possible, but hardly probable. Goya lived completely isolated in his own world, and it is difficult to believe that he would feel anxious to mix with the French painters who, although his contemporaries, were so distant from him in their outlook on the world and mankind, though there may have been some passing contacts. In his long hours of silence, Goya carried on painting and drawing.

Fig. 132

September found Goya settled in Bordeaux, reunited with Leocadia Zorrilla and her children, Guillermo and Rosario Weiss. In a letter dated on the eighteenth of this month, Moratín wrote: "Goya is now with the lady and the children in a nice furnished place and in good health. I think he will be able to spend the winter there very comfortably. He wants to paint my portrait, and from this you will gather how well I look, if such able brushes wish to make replicas of me."

The general impression of Goya's life at this time, however, is a sad one, and although his life had not been a succession of happiness, it does seem that a constant dissatisfaction now began to weigh upon him more heavily every day. Calling upon his unconquerable will and energy, and upon that second nature that long habit and experience in one's profession bring in maturity, he embarked on the series of drawings that constitute one of the most remarkable phenomena in the history of art, as much for their humanity as for their technique, a restless technique that seems to anticipate every bold technical innovation of the future. He was also to start on the series of paintings on ivory which represents a new and distinct aspect of Goya's art in his last years.

On 7th January 1825, the Royal leave of absence having expired, Goya belatedly applied for its renewal. In his application he ingenuously gives as the reason his need to take the waters at another spa, Bagnières. The Madrid authorities evidently decided to treat his request with indulgence, in view of his advanced age and exceptional talents, for it is pretty certain that his real motives were understood. Goya's fears of political reprisal must have been more imaginary than real. Who could have feared anything of a poor and aged deaf man? The extension of his leave of absence from his duties as *Pintor de Cámara* was sent to him by return of post.

The following letter from Moratín, written on 14th April of this year, is of considerable interest and charm: "Goya, with his seventy-nine flourishing birthdays and his complaints, does not know what to hope for nor what he wants; I have urged him to be quiet until his leave is finished. He enjoys the town, the countryside, the climate, the food, the freedom and the tranquillity that is granted him. Since he has been here he has not had any of the illnesses that troubled him over there, and yet at times he gets it into his head that there is much for him to do in Madrid; and if they let him, he would take the road on a vicious mule, with his cap and cloak, his walnut stirrups, his wineskin and his saddle bags."

In the peaceful environment of Bordeaux Goya's restlessness was to return. He would like to go back to Madrid, and he forgets his past hours of anguish, disillusionment and fear. But a new illness thwarts his desire. He suffers from an attack of paralysis of the bladder and a tumour on the perineum, and according to his doctor the illness is serious. But Moratín's letters, keeping up with events, tell us that in the middle of June Goya was convalescing and painting, "without wanting to correct anything he paints". We also learn from Moratín's correspondence that Goya was now living in a small house with a garden, with Leocadia Zorrilla and the little Rosario, who was by now chatting to her friends in French (letter of 30th October).

His friendship with Gaulon, a printer of Bordeaux, led Goya to make some lithographs, a technique he had already tried in Madrid. His lithographic works in Bordeaux are restricted to a very few plates, among which are the two magnificent *Portraits of Gaulon and his Son*. But of special interest for us are the four plates known under the title *Los Toros de Burdeos* (The Bulls of Bordeaux), which comprise the following titles: *The famous American Mariano Ceballos, Picador caught by a bull, Spanish entertainment* and *Division of the Arena or Divided Arena*.

Figs. 128 to 131

In a letter dated 7th May 1826, Moratín announces Goya's departure for Madrid: "He left, alone and little pleased with the French... If he does not arrive, do not be surprised, for the slightest little upset could leave him cold in the corner of some hostelry"; a very understandable view, bearing in mind Goya's eighty years, his ill health and his anxieties.

On arriving in Madrid the painter requested to be relieved of his court duties. On the 17th of this same month his request was granted, with the payment of his salary up to date and with permission to return to France. The Valencian Vicente López, who in Goya's absence had become the fashionable painter of Madrid, was at the time *First Painter to the Chamber*. His series of portraits of members of the Court and contemporary high society is in perfect accord with this period of ostentatious mediocrity. It was on this occasion that López painted the famous portrait of Goya,

29

now in the Prado. Tradition relates that the aged painter restrained his successor from giving the portrait that excessive finish which characterizes López's paintings.

Neither his son nor his grandson was able to hold Goya in Madrid, and he soon journeyed back to Bordeaux, where he arrived in July. Moratín writes: "Goya is well, and passes his time with his sketching; he takes his stroll, dines, and takes his *siesta*; it seems to me there is tranquillity in his house now." The "sketches" refer almost certainly to the remarkable series of drawings he was doing in these years of exile, the greater number executed in black chalk. In these drawings he recorded all that he saw or that might attract his attention on his strolls or at the circus, to which he would take Rosario Weiss, now twelve years of age. One of the drawings, representing a very lean man and bearing the legend *Living skeleton*, is dated in Bordeaux in 1826.

Goya had now passed his eightieth birthday, a fact he records on a painting signed and dated in this year: *"Don Santiago Galos, painted by Goya, at the age of eighty years, in 1826."* Galos was Goya's banker. In a letter to his son, the painter remarks: "You know what Marianito [Goya's grandson] has in Galos' house."

The works dated in the year 1827 show that Goya was still painting with determination and with a clear mind: the portrait of *Juan Muguiro* does not betray any decay in the artist's faculties. *Fig. 133*

Finally, there are those deservedly famous paintings, *The Milkmaid of Bordeaux*, which is *Fig. 135* actually a portrait of the girl who delivered Goya's milk on her mule, and the portrait of *José Pío* *Fig. 134* *de Molina*, who had been Mayor of Madrid under the Constitution. These last two paintings have always been considered the last works Goya painted; and the portrait of *Pío de Molina*, always regarded as left unfinished at his death, could well have been painted early in 1828. It will have been observed that in this last phase of his art, that is, from the time of the miniatures on ivory, Goya leaves themes of fantasy and concerns himself with immediate reality, painting portraits and making drawings that record his observation of the present reality around him, of scenes of the circus, animals, etc., culminating in the beautiful painting of the *Milkmaid*, with which the artist so fittingly bids his "farewell" to the beautiful in the world, and which without hesitation we pronounce one of his finest paintings.

A letter from Goya to his son, dated 17th January 1828, appears to have been written just before the onset of another very serious illness, serious enough to decide his daughter-in-law and grandson to undertake the journey to Bordeaux. In another letter, dated 12th March, Goya writes to Javier: "I was overwhelmed with joy to receive your last letter..." and continues, with his incomparable optimism, referring to his son's anticipated visit: "...that you come and stay a couple of years, when you like, and I shall be very happy."

Mariano and his mother arrived on 28th March. Three days later Goya adds a few lines to a letter that Mariano had written to his father, and they were to be the last words he ever wrote: "Dear Javier, I cannot tell you any more than that, from so much happiness, I am a little indisposed and in bed. May God grant that I see you come to join them [Javier's wife and son], and then my happiness will be complete. Adios, your father, Frco."

On the following day, 2nd April, Goya had lost his power of speech and was in a state of semi-paralysis which was to last for thirteen days. He died during the night of the 15th-16th April, attended at his bedside by Pío de Molina and Brugada, the painter who used to accompany him on his last strolls.

He was laid to rest in the Bordeaux cemetery, in a small burial vault in which another Spanish refugee lay at rest, a Martín Miguel de Goicoechea, one of the countless persons bearing this Basque name. On 29th November 1919 the mingled remains of both were transferred to Spain and buried in the hermitage of San Antonio de la Florida, under the splendid frescoes that Goya had painted at the peak of his artistic career and the height of his glory. In 1927 Goya's first tomb was transferred to Zaragoza, where it is still preserved.

The details of the great painter's death are recounted in a letter of 28th April 1828, written by Doña Leocadia to Moratín in Paris, which we quote: "The grandson and daughter-in-law arrived here on the 28th of last month, and on the 1st we ate together; the meal made him ill and on the 2nd, his day of days (the Day of Saint Francis de Paul, Goya's saint's day), he was unable to speak until five o'clock, when he recovered his speech, and became paralyzed in his side. He remained like this for thirteen days; he recognized everyone up to three hours before he died; he could see his hand, but seemed bewildered; he wanted to make a will, he said, in our favour, and his daughter-in-law told him he had already made it. After this there was not a clear moment, for his weakness obstructed what little appreciation he might have had of what she was saying and babbling... He died on the 15th to 16th at two in the morning... Molina and Brugada saw him die, and I was in the room until two minutes before; but from twelve o'clock I did not have the strength to stay at his bedside... at half past twelve (before, she had said at two o'clock) he passed away; so peaceful, and he looked like someone sleeping, and even the doctor was amazed at his endurance; he says that he could not have suffered anything; I am not sure."

ABRIDGED BIBLIOGRAPHY

ÁGUEDA, M. and SALAS, X. DE: *Francisco de Goya. Cartas a Martín Zapater.* Madrid, 1982.

ANGULO IÑÍGUEZ, D.: *La familia del Infante Don Luis, pintada por Goya.* "Archivo Español de Arte". Vol. XIV, pp. 49-58. Madrid, 1962.
El Saturno y las pinturas negras de Goya. "Archivo Español de Arte". Vol. XXXV, No. 138, pp. 173-177. Madrid, 1962.

BERUETE Y MORET, A. DE: *Goya, pintor de retratos.* Madrid, 1916.
Goya, composiciones y figuras. Madrid, 1917.
Goya, grabador. Madrid, 1918.

CAMÓN AZNAR, J.: *"Los Disparates" de Goya y sus dibujos preparatorios.* Barcelona, 1951.
Francisco de Goya. Zaragoza, 1980-82.

CANELLAS LÓPEZ, A.: *Francisco de Goya. Diplomatario.* Zaragoza, 1981.

DESPARMET FITZ-GÉRALD, X.: *L'œuvre peint de Goya. Catalogue raisonné.* Paris, 1928-1950.

EZQUERRA DEL BAYO, J.: *La Duquesa de Alba y Goya.* Madrid, 1928.

GALINDO, P.: *Goya pintando en el Pilar.* Aragon, 1928.

GASSIER, P.: *Dibujos de Goya.* Fribourg/Barcelona, 1973 and 1975.

GASSIER, P. and WILSON, J.: *Vie et œuvre de Francisco Goya.* Fribourg, 1970.

GUDIOL, J.: *Les peintures de Goya dans la chartreuse d'Aula Dei à Saragosse.* "Gazette des Beaux-Arts" VI period, Vol. LVII, No. 1105, pp. 83-94. Paris, February 1961.
Francisco Goya. Biografía, estudio analítico y catálogo de sus pinturas. Barcelona, 1970.
Francisco Goya. Biografía, estudio analítico y catálogo de sus pinturas. Barcelona, 1980.

HARRIS, T.: *Goya. Engravings and lithographs.* Oxford, 1964.

LAFUENTE FERRARI, E.: *Goya. El Dos de Mayo y los fusilamientos.* Barcelona, 1946.
Antecedentes, coincidencias e influencias del arte de Goya. Catalogue of the exhibition held by the "Amigos del Arte", Madrid, 1947.
Los "Desastres de la Guerra", de Goya, y sus dibujos preparatorios. Barcelona, 1952.
Goya: les fresques de San Antonio de la Florida à Madrid. Lausanne, 1955.

MAYER, A. L.: *Francisco de Goya.* Munich. Spanish translation. Madrid, 1923.

MILICUA, J.: *Anotaciones al Goya joven.* "Paragone" No. 53, pp. 5-28. Florence, May 1954.

SALAS, X. DE: *La familia de Carlos IV.* Barcelona, 1944.
Sur les tableaux de Goya qui appartinrent à son fils. "Gazette des Beaux-Arts", IV period, Vol. LXIII, No. 1141, pp. 99-110. Paris, February 1964.
Goya. Milan, 1978.

SAMBRICIO, V. DE: *Tapices de Goya.* Madrid, 1946.
Los retratos de Carlos IV y María Luisa, por Goya. "Archivo Español de Arte", Vol. XXX, pp. 85-113. Madrid, 1957.

SÁNCHEZ CANTÓN, F. J.: *Los "Caprichos" de Goya y sus dibujos preparatorios.* Barcelona, 1949.
Goya, su vida y sus obras. Madrid, 1953.
Escultura y pintura del siglo XVIII, Francisco Goya. Ars Hispaniae, Vol. XVII. Madrid, 1958.

SÁNCHEZ CANTÓN, F. J. and SALAS, X. DE: *Goya y sus pinturas negras en la Quinta del Sordo.* Milan-Barcelona, 1963.

SORIA, M. S.: *Agustín Esteve y Goya.* Valencia, 1957.

VIÑAZA, CONDE DE LA: *Goya. Su tiempo, su vida, sus obras.* Madrid, 1887.

YRIARTE, CH.: *Goya.* Paris, 1867.

ZAPATER Y GÓMEZ, F.: *Goya, noticias biográficas.* Zaragoza, 1868.

1. *Paintings of the Reliquary in the Parish Church of Fuendetodos* (Zaragoza). *c.* 1762. (Destroyed in 1936.)

2. *Sacrifice to Vesta*. 1771.
Oil on canvas, 33×24 cm.
Private collection, Barcelona.

3. *Visitation of the Blessed Virgin to Saint Elizabeth* (detail of the mural painting). 1774.
Oil on canvas, 306×790 cm.
Church of the Carthusian house of Aula Dei, Zaragoza.

3

4. *Adoration of the Name of God by the Angels.* 1772.
(Sketch for the Coreto fresco of the Basilica of El Pilar, Zaragoza.)
Oil on canvas, 75 × 152 cm.
Private collection, Barcelona.

5. *Self-Portrait. c.* 1773.
Oil on canvas, 58 × 44 cm.
Private collection, Madrid.

6. *The Maja and the Men in Cloaks.* 1777.
(Tapestry cartoon.)
Oil on canvas, 275 × 190 cm.
Prado Museum, Madrid.

6

7

7. *The Dance on the Banks of the Manzanares.* 1777.
(Tapestry cartoon.)
Oil on canvas, 272×295 cm.
Prado Museum, Madrid.

8-9. *The Picnic.* 1776.
(Tapestry cartoon.)
Oil on canvas, 272×295 cm.
Prado Museum, Madrid.

8

9

10-11. *The Parasol.* 1777.
(Tapestry cartoon.)
Oil on canvas, 104 × 152 cm.
Prado Museum, Madrid.

10

12. *The Fight at the Cock Inn.* 1777.
(Sketch for the tapestry cartoon.)
Oil on canvas, 40×65 cm.
Private collection, Paris.

13-14. *The Fight at the New Inn.* 1777.
(Tapestry cartoon.)
Oil on canvas, 275×414 cm.
Prado Museum, Madrid.

12

13

15-16. *The Crockery Vendor.* 1779.
(Tapestry cartoon.)
Oil on canvas, 259×220 cm.
Prado Museum, Madrid.

17. *Game of Bat and Ball.* 1779.
(Sketch for the tapestry cartoon.)
Oil on canvas.
Private collection.

18-19. *Game of Bat and Ball.* 1779.
(Tapestry cartoon.)
Oil on canvas, 261 × 470 cm.
Prado Museum, Madrid.

17

18

19

20-21. *The Washerwomen*. 1779.
(Tapestry cartoon.)
Oil on canvas, 218 × 166 cm.
Prado Museum, Madrid.

21

22

22. *Christ Crucified*. 1780.
Oil on canvas, 255 × 153 cm.
Prado Museum, Madrid.

23. *Francisco Bayeu. c.* 1780.
Oil on canvas, 49 × 35 cm.
Private collection, Barcelona.

23

24

25

26

27

24-25. *Regina Martyrum*. 1780.
(Sketch of fresco painting for
the dome of the Basilica of
El Pilar in Zaragoza.)
Oil on canvas, 85 × 165 cm.
El Pilar Museum, Zaragoza.

26. *Regina Martyrum*. 1780.
(Sketch of fresco painting for
the dome of the Basilica of
El Pilar in Zaragoza.)
Oil on canvas, 85 × 165 cm.
El Pilar Museum, Zaragoza.

27. *Regina Martyrum*. 1780-1781.
Fresco painting.
Dome of the Basilica of El Pilar,
Zaragoza.

28

28. *Preaching of Saint Bernardino of Siena.* 1782-1783.
Oil on canvas, 480×300 cm.
Church of San Francisco el Grande, Madrid.

29. *Maria Teresa de Vallabriga.* 1783.
Oil on canvas, 148×93 cm.
Alte Pinakothek, Munich.

29

30

31

32

30-31. *María Teresa de Borbón y Vallabriga. Condesa de Chinchón.* 1783.
Oil on canvas, 130 × 116 cm.
National Gallery, Washington.

32. *Luis María de Borbón y Vallabriga.* 1783.
Oil on canvas, 130 × 116 cm.
Private collection, Madrid.

33. *José Moñino. Conde de Floridablanca.* 1783.
Oil on canvas, 260 × 166 cm.
Banco Urquijo, Madrid.

34. *Gaspar Melchor de Jovellanos. c.* 1784-1785.
Oil on canvas, 185×110 cm.
Private collection, Barcelona.

35. *The Duchess of Osuna.* 1785.
Oil on canvas, 104×80 cm.
Private collection, Palma de Mallorca.

36-37. *Francisco Bayeu.* 1786.
Oil on canvas, 107×80 cm.
Museum of Fine Arts, Valencia.

35

36

37

38

39

38. *The Threshing-Ground*. 1786-1787.
(Sketch for tapestry cartoon.)
Oil on canvas, 34 × 76 cm.
Lázaro Galdiano Museum, Madrid.

39-40. *The Grape-Harvest*. 1786-1787.
(Tapestry cartoon.)
Oil on canvas, 275 × 190 cm.
Prado Museum, Madrid.

41

41. *The Flower-Sellers.* 1786-1787.
(Tapestry cartoon.)
Oil on canvas, 277 × 192 cm.
Prado Museum, Madrid.

42. *The Wounded Mason.* 1786-1787.
(Tapestry cartoon.)
Oil on canvas, 268 × 110 cm.
Prado Museum, Madrid.

43

43. *Manuel Osorio Manrique de Zúñiga.* 1788.
Oil on canvas, 110 × 80 cm.
Metropolitan Museum, New York.

44-45. *The Meadow of San Isidro.* 1788.
(Sketch for a tapestry cartoon which was not carried out.)
Oil on canvas, 44 × 94 cm.
Prado Museum , Madrid.

46. *The Hermitage of San Isidro.* 1788.
Oil on canvas, 42 × 44 cm.
Prado Museum, Madrid.

44

45

46

47. *Saint Francis of Borja Attending a Dying Man.* 1788.
(Sketch for the work in fig. 48.)
Oil on canvas, 37×26 cm.
Private collection, Madrid.

48. *Saint Francis of Borja Attending a Dying Man* (detail). 1788.
Oil on canvas, 350×300 cm.
Cathedral of Valencia.

48

49. *The Duke and Duchess of Osuna with their Children.* 1788.
Oil on canvas, 255 × 174 cm.
Prado Museum, Madrid.

50-51. *The Little Giants.* 1791-1792.
(Tapestry cartoon.)
Oil on canvas, 137 × 104 cm.
Private collection, Madrid.

50

51

52. *The Fire.* 1793-1794.
Oil on a sheet of tin, 50×32 cm.
Private collection, Madrid.

53. *The Madhouse Yard.* 1794.
Oil on a sheet of tin, 46×31 cm.
Meadows Museum, Dallas, Texas.

53

54. *The Duchess of Alba.* 1795.
Oil on canvas, 194 × 130 cm.
Private collection, Madrid.

55. *The Duchess of Alba.* 1797.
Oil on canvas, 210 × 148 cm.
Hispanic Society, New York.

56

56. *Witches' Sabbath c.* 1795-1798.
Oil on canvas, 43 × 30 cm.
Lázaro Galdiano Museum, Madrid.

57. *The Bullfighter Pedro Romero.*
c. 1796-1798.
Oil on canvas, 85 × 64 cm.
Private collection, Zürich.

58. *Fighting Bull. c.* 1796-1798.
Oil on canvas, 75 × 80 cm.
Private collection, Barcelona.

57

58

59 to 62. *Miracle of Saint Anthony of Padua.* 1798.
Fresco paintings.
Dome of the Hermitage of San Antonio de la Florida, Madrid.

59

60

61

63

63. *Queen Maria Luisa.* 1799.
Oil on canvas, 335 × 279 cm.
Prado Museum, Madrid.

64-65. *Carlos IV.* 1799.
Oil on canvas, 305 × 279 cm.
Prado Museum, Madrid.

64

66. *The Condesa de Chinchón*. 1800.
Oil on canvas, 216×144 cm.
Private collection, Madrid.

67. *Self-portrait*. 1800.
Oil on canvas, 61×47 cm.
Museum of Castres.

67

68 to 70. *The Family of Carlos IV.* 1800.
Oil on canvas, 280 × 336 cm.
Prado Museum, Madrid.

68

69

71

72

73

74

71-72. *Manuel Godoy*. 1801.
Oil on canvas, 187×268 cm.
Academy of San Fernando, Madrid.

73. *The Conde de Fernán Núñez*. 1803.
Oil on canvas, 200×122 cm.
Private collection, Madrid.

74. *The Duchess of Montellano, Condesa de Fernán Núñez*. 1803.
Oil on canvas, 200×122 cm.
Private collection, Madrid.

75. *The Marqués de San Adrián.* 1804.
Oil on canvas, 209×127 cm.
Provincial Council of Navarra.

76-77. *The Marquesa de Santa Cruz.* 1805.
Oil on canvas, 130×210 cm.
County Museum, Los Angeles.

76

77

78. *Isabel Cobos de Porcel.* 1806.
Oil on canvas, 82 × 55 cm.
National Gallery, London.

79. *Sabasa García. c.* 1803-1806.
Oil on canvas, 71 × 58 cm.
National Gallery, Washington.

80. *Psyche and Cupid. c.* 1803-1806.
Oil on canvas, 221 × 156 cm.
Cambó Collection, Palau de la Virreina, Barcelona.

79

80

81

82

81. *The Clothed Maja. c.* 1803-1806.
Oil on canvas, 95 × 190 cm.
Prado Museum, Madrid.

82-83. *The Naked Maja. c.* 1803-1806.
Oil on canvas, 97 × 190 cm.
Prado Museum, Madrid.

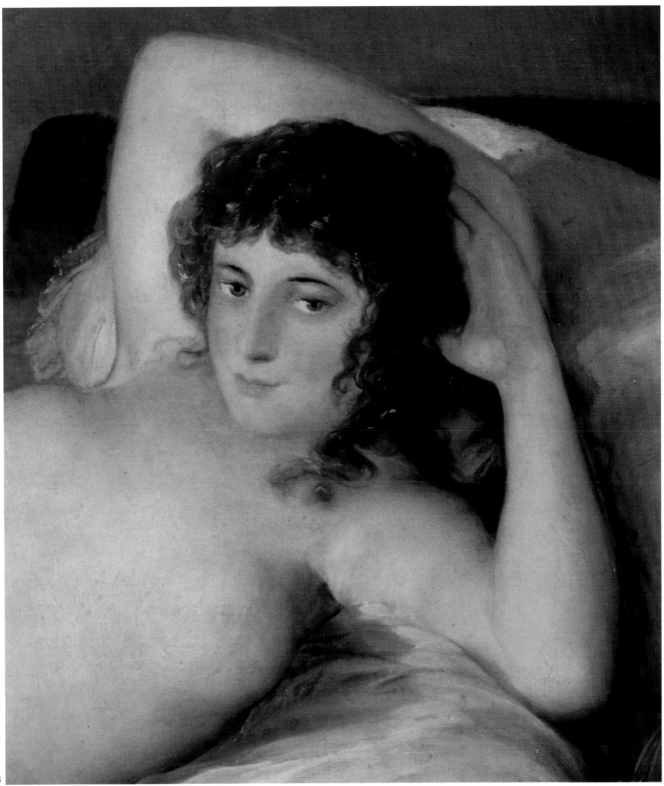

84. *Tribunal of the Inquisition. c.* 1803-1806.
Oil on wooden panel, 45×72 cm.
Academy of San Fernando, Madrid.

85-86. *Flagellants. c.* 1803-1806.
Oil on wooden panel, 45×73 cm.
Academy of San Fernando, Madrid.

84

85

87. *Madhouse. c.* 1803-1806.
Oil on wooden panel, 45×72 cm.
Academy of San Fernando, Madrid.

88-89. *Bullfight. c.* 1803-1806.
Oil on wooden panel, 45×72 cm.
Academy of San Fernando, Madrid.

87

88

90. *Burial of the Sardine. c.* 1803-1806.
Oil on wooden panel, 83 × 62 cm.
Academy of San Fernando, Madrid.

91. *Víctor Guye* (detail). 1810.
Oil on canvas, 108 × 86 cm.
National Gallery of Art, Washington.

92. *The "Lazarillo de Tormes"* (detail). *c.* 1808-1812.
Oil on canvas, 80 × 65 cm.
Private collection, Madrid.

91

92

93

93. *Majas on a Balcony. c.* 1805-1812.
Oil on canvas, 192 × 127 cm.
Metropolitan Museum, New York.

94. *The Letter. c.* 1808-1812.
Oil on canvas, 181 × 122 cm.
Museum of Fine Arts, Lille.

95. *Until Death. c.* 1808-1812.
Oil on canvas, 181 × 125 cm.
Museum of Fine Arts, Lille.

96. *A Giant. c.* 1810-1812.
Oil on canvas, 116 × 105 cm.
Prado Museum, Madrid.

97

98

97. *It's a hard step.* 1808-1814.
(No. 14 in the series *The Disasters of War.*)
Etching, 15.5 × 16.5 cm.
Prado Museum, Madrid.

98. *The Horrors of War.* 1808-1814.
(No. 30 in the series *The Disasters of War.*)
Etching, 14 × 17 cm.
Prado Museum, Madrid.

99. *And They Are Beasts.* 1808-1814.
(No. 5 in the series *The Disasters of War.*)
Etching, 15.5 × 21 cm.
Prado Museum, Madrid.

100. *One Can't Look.* 1808-1814.
(No. 26 in the series *The Disasters of War.*)
Etching, 14.5 × 21 cm.
Prado Museum, Madrid.

99

100

101

101. *General José de Palafox*. 1814.
Oil on canvas, 248 × 224 cm.
Prado Museum, Madrid.

102-103. *The Second of May 1808,
in Madrid: The Attack on
the Mamelukes*. 1814.
Oil on canvas, 266 × 345 cm.
Prado Museum, Madrid.

102

104-105. *The Third of May 1808, in Madrid: The Executions on Prince Pio's Hill.* 1814.
Oil on canvas, 266 × 345 cm.
Prado Museum, Madrid.

106

107

106. *Ignacio de Omulryan* (detail). 1815.
Oil on canvas, 84×63 cm.
William Rockhill Nelson Gallery of Art, Kansas City.

107. *Fray Juan Fernández de Rojas. c.* 1815.
Oil on canvas, 75×54 cm.
Academia de la Historia, Madrid.

108-109. *Fernando VII.* 1815.
Oil on canvas, 215×150 cm.
Museum of Fine Arts, Zaragoza.

108

111

112

110. *Self-Portrait*. 1815.
Oil on wooden panel, 44 × 40 cm.
Academy of San Fernando, Madrid.

111. *The Duke of San Carlos* (detail). 1815.
Oil on canvas, 280 × 125 cm.
Museum of Fine Arts, Zaragoza.

112. *The Engraver Rafael Esteve* (detail). 1815.
Oil on canvas, 98 × 75 cm.
Museum of Fine Arts, Valencia.

113

113. *"El Empecinado."* c. 1815.
Oil on canvas, 84 × 65 cm.
Private collection, Cologne.

114. *The Tenth Duke of Osuna.* 1816.
Oil on canvas, 202 × 140 cm.
Bonnat Museum, Bayonne.

115. *The Duchess of Abrantes.* 1816.
Oil on canvas, 92 × 71 cm.
Private collection, Madrid.

116. *The Last Communion of Saint Joseph of Calasanz.* 1819.
Oil on canvas, 250 × 180 cm.
Church of San Antonio Abad, Madrid.

114

115

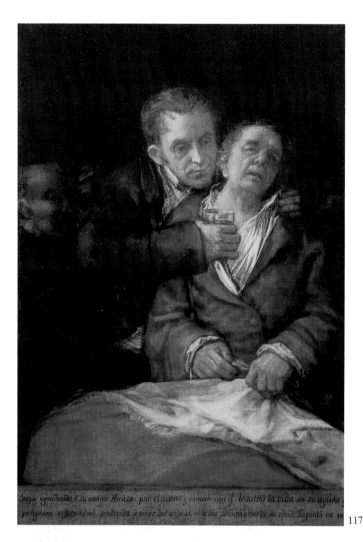

117

118

117. *Goya Being Attended by Arrieta.* 1820.
Oil on canvas, 115 × 80 cm.
Institute of Arts, Minneapolis.

118. *José Duaso y Latre.* 1824.
Oil on canvas, 74 × 59 cm.
Private collection, Madrid.

119. *La Leocadia.* 1821-1822.
(Quinta del Sordo.)
Oil on canvas, 147 × 132 cm.
Prado Museum, Madrid.

120. *Saturn*. 1821-1822.
(Quinta del Sordo.)
Oil on canvas, 146 × 83 cm.
Prado Museum, Madrid.

121-122. *Two Strangers*. 1821-1822.
(Quinta del Sordo.)
Oil on canvas, 123 × 266 cm.
Prado Museum, Madrid.

120

121

123-124. *Asmodée.* 1821-1822.
(Quinta del Sordo.)
Oil on canvas, 123 × 265 cm.
Prado Museum, Madrid.

125-126. *The Great He-Goat.* 1821-1822.
(Quinta del Sordo.)
Oil on canvas, 140 × 438 cm.
Prado Museum, Madrid.

123

124

125

126

127

128

127. *Group of Old Folk*. 1823-1824.
Oil on wooden panel, 31 × 20 cm.
Alte Pinakothek, Munich.

128-129. *Spanish Entertainment. c.* 1825.
Oil on canvas, 46 × 58 cm.
Ashmolean Museum, Oxford.

130-131. *Picador Caught by a Bull. c.* 1824.
Oil on canvas, 64×93 cm.
Museum of Art, Toledo, Ohio (USA).

130

132

133

134

132. *Leandro Fernández de Moratín.* 1824.
Oil on canvas, 60 × 49 cm.
Museum of Fine Arts, Bilbao.

133. *Juan Bautista de Muguiro* (detail). 1827.
Oil on canvas, 101 × 89 cm.
Prado Museum, Madrid.

134. *José Pío de Molina.* 1827.
Oil on canvas, 60 × 50 cm.
Oscar Reinhart Foundation, Winterthur.

135. *The Milkmaid of Bordeaux. c.* 1827.
Oil on canvas, 74 × 68 cm.
Prado Museum, Madrid.

INDEX OF ILLUSTRATIONS

64-65. *Carlos IV.* 1799.
Oil on canvas, 305 × 279 cm.
Prado Museum, Madrid.

66. *The Condesa de Chinchón.* 1800.
Oil on canvas, 216 × 144 cm.
Private collection, Madrid.

67. *Self-portrait.* 1800.
Oil on canvas, 61 × 47 cm.
Museum of Castres.

68 to 70. *The Family of Carlos IV.* 1800.
Oil on canvas, 280 × 336 cm.
Prado Museum, Madrid.

71-72. *Manuel Godoy.* 1801.
Oil on canvas, 187 × 268 cm.
Academy of San Fernando, Madrid.

73. *The Conde de Fernán Núñez.* 1803.
Oil on canvas, 200 × 122 cm.
Private collection, Madrid.

74. *The Duchess of Montellano, Condesa de Fernán Núñez.* 1803.
Oil on canvas, 200 × 122 cm.
Private collection, Madrid.

75. *The Marqués de San Adrián.* 1804.
Oil on canvas, 209 × 127 cm.
Provincial Council of Navarra.

76-77. *The Marquesa de Santa Cruz.* 1805.
Oil on canvas, 130 × 210 cm.
County Museum, Los Angeles.

78. *Isabel Cobos de Porcel.* 1806.
Oil on canvas, 82 × 55 cm.
National Gallery, London.

79. *Sabasa García.* c. 1803-1806.
Oil on canvas, 71 × 58 cm.
National Gallery, Washington.

80. *Psyche and Cupid.* c. 1803-1806.
Oil on canvas, 221 × 156 cm.
Cambó Collection, Palau de la Virreina, Barcelona.

81. *The Clothed Maja.* c. 1803-1806.
Oil on canvas, 95 × 190 cm.
Prado Museum, Madrid.

82-83. *The Naked Maja.* c. 1803-1806.
Oil on canvas, 97 × 190 cm.
Prado Museum, Madrid.

84. *Tribunal of the Inquisition.* c. 1803-1806.
Oil on wooden panel, 45 × 72 cm.
Academy of San Fernando, Madrid.

85-86. *Flagellants.* c. 1803-1806.
Oil on wooden panel, 45 × 73 cm.
Academy of San Fernando, Madrid.

87. *Madhouse.* c. 1803-1806.
Oil on wooden panel, 45 × 72 cm.
Academy of San Fernando, Madrid.

88-89. *Bullfight.* c. 1803-1806.
Oil on wooden panel, 45 × 72 cm.
Academy of San Fernando, Madrid.

90. *Burial of the Sardine.* c. 1803-1806.
Oil on wooden panel, 83 × 62 cm.
Academy of San Fernando, Madrid.

91. *Víctor Guye* (detail). 1810.
Oil on canvas, 108 × 86 cm.
National Gallery of Art, Washington.

92. *The "Lazarillo de Tormes"* (detail). c. 1808-1812.
Oil on canvas, 80 × 65 cm.
Private collection, Madrid.

93. *Majas on a Balcony.* c. 1805-1812.
Oil on canvas, 192 × 127 cm.
Metropolitan Museum, New York.

94. *The Letter.* c. 1808-1812.
Oil on canvas, 181 × 122 cm.
Museum of Fine Arts, Lille.

95. *Until Death.* c. 1808-1812.
Oil on canvas, 181 × 125 cm.
Museum of Fine Arts, Lille.

96. *A Giant.* c. 1810-1812.
Oil on canvas, 116 × 105 cm.
Prado Museum, Madrid.

97. *It's a hard step.* 1808-1814.
(No. 14 in the series *The Disasters of War.*)
Etching, 15.5 × 16.5 cm.
Prado Museum, Madrid.

98. *The Horrors of War.* 1808-1814.
(No. 30 in the series *The Disasters of War.*)
Etching, 14 × 17 cm.
Prado Museum, Madrid.

99. *And They Are Beasts.* 1808-1814.
(No. 5 in the series *The Disasters of War.*)
Etching, 15.5 × 21 cm.
Prado Museum, Madrid.

100. *One Can't Look.* 1808-1814.
(No. 26 in the series *The Disasters of War.*)
Etching, 14.5 × 21 cm.
Prado Museum, Madrid.

101. *General José de Palafox.* 1814.
Oil on canvas, 248 × 224 cm.
Prado Museum, Madrid.

102-103. *The Second of May 1808, in Madrid: The Attack on the Mamelukes.* 1814.
Oil on canvas, 266 × 345 cm.
Prado Museum, Madrid.

104-105. *The Third of May 1808, in Madrid: The Executions on Prince Pio's Hill.* 1814.
Oil on canvas, 266 × 345 cm.
Prado Museum, Madrid.

106. *Ignacio de Omulryan* (detail). 1815.
Oil on canvas, 84 × 63 cm.
William Rockhill Nelson Gallery of Art, Kansas City.

107. *Fray Juan Fernández de Rojas.* c. 1815.
Oil on canvas, 75 × 54 cm.
Academia de la Historia, Madrid.

108-109. *Fernando VII.* 1815.
Oil on canvas, 215 × 150 cm.
Museum of Fine Arts, Zaragoza.

110. *Self-Portrait.* 1815.
Oil on wooden panel, 44 × 40 cm.
Academy of San Fernando, Madrid.

111. *The Duke of San Carlos* (detail). 1815.
Oil on canvas, 280 × 125 cm.
Museum of Fine Arts, Zaragoza.

112. *The Engraver Rafael Esteve* (detail). 1815.
Oil on canvas, 98 × 75 cm.
Museum of Fine Arts, Valencia.

113. *"El Empecinado."* c. 1815.
Oil on canvas, 84 × 65 cm.
Private collection, Cologne.

114. *The Tenth Duke of Osuna.* 1816.
Oil on canvas, 202 × 140 cm.
Bonnat Museum, Bayonne.

115. *The Duchess of Abrantes.* 1816.
Oil on canvas, 92 × 71 cm.
Private collection, Madrid.

116. *The Last Communion of Saint Joseph of Calasanz.* 1819.
Oil on canvas, 250 × 180 cm.
Church of San Antonio Abad, Madrid.

117. *Goya Being Attended by Arrieta.* 1820.
Oil on canvas, 115 × 80 cm.
Institute of Arts, Minneapolis.

118. *José Duaso y Latre.* 1824.
Oil on canvas, 74 × 59 cm.
Private collection, Madrid.

119. *La Leocadia.* 1821-1822. *(Quinta del Sordo.)*
Oil on canvas, 147 × 132 cm.
Prado Museum, Madrid.

120. *Saturn.* 1821-1822. *(Quinta del Sordo.)*
Oil on canvas, 146 × 83 cm.
Prado Museum, Madrid.

121-122. *Two Strangers.* 1821-1822. *(Quinta del Sordo.)*
Oil on canvas, 123 × 266 cm.
Prado Museum, Madrid.

123-124. *Asmodée.* 1821-1822. *(Quinta del Sordo.)*
Oil on canvas, 123 × 265 cm.
Prado Museum, Madrid.

125-126. *The Great He-Goat.* 1821-1822. *(Quinta del Sordo.)*
Oil on canvas, 140 × 438 cm.
Prado Museum, Madrid.

127. *Group of Old Folk.* 1823-1824.
Oil on wooden panel, 31 × 20 cm.
Alte Pinakothek, Munich.

128-129. *Spanish Entertainment.* c. 1825.
Oil on canvas, 46 × 58 cm.
Ashmolean Museum, Oxford.

130-131. *Picador Caught by a Bull.* c. 1824.
Oil on canvas, 64 × 93 cm.
Museum of Art, Toledo, Ohio (USA).

132. *Leandro Fernández de Moratín.* 1824.
Oil on canvas, 60 × 49 cm.
Museum of Fine Arts, Bilbao.

133. *Juan Bautista de Muguiro* (detail). 1827.
Oil on canvas, 101 × 89 cm.
Prado Museum, Madrid.

134. *José Pío de Molina.* 1827.
Oil on canvas, 60 × 50 cm.
Oscar Reinhart Foundation, Winterthur.

135. *The Milkmaid of Bordeaux.* c. 1827.
Oil on canvas, 74 × 68 cm.
Prado Museum, Madrid.